Functional Skills
Maths – Level 2
Revision Guide

Improving understanding through colour and clarity

Get your FREE digital book!

This book includes a free digital edition for use on computers (PC and Mac), tablets or smartphones.

Go to ddedu.co.uk/maths-fsl2
and enter this code...

Code: DPPBRO40

Functional Skills **Maths**

Contents

Maths Jargon

Integers

0	120	5	−73	−394	88

Integers are whole numbers, including zero and negative numbers.

Prime Numbers

2	17	5	19	67	13	79	19

Prime numbers have only 2 factors, themselves and 1.

Prime factors are factors which are also prime numbers. For example, 2 and 3 are prime factors of 12.

Multiples

Every number has **multiples**. For example, every number that 3 goes into is a **multiple** of 3, so **3, 6, 9, 12, 15, 18**... etc. are all multiples of 3.

The **lowest common multiple (LCM)** of two numbers is the smallest whole number which is a multiple of both numbers.

The **LCM of 4 and 10 is 20**:

Multiples of 4: 4, 8, 12, 16, **20**, 24

Multiples of 10: 10, **20**, 30, 40, 50

Factors

Every number has **factors**. The factors of **12** are **1, 2, 3, 4, 6** and **12** because all of these numbers go exactly into 12.

The **highest common factor (HCF)** of two numbers is the largest whole number which is a factor of both numbers.

The **HCF of 18 and 30 is 6**:

Factors of 18: 1, 2, 3, **6**, 9, 18

Factors of 30: 1, 2, 3, 5, **6**, 10, 15, 30

Squares & Cubes

1^2
$1 \times 1 = 1$

2^2
$2 \times 2 = 4$

3^2
$3 \times 3 = 9$

A **square number** is the product of a number multiplied by itself.

1^3
$1 \times 1 \times 1 = 1$

2^3
$2 \times 2 \times 2 = 8$

3^3
$3 \times 3 \times 3 = 27$

A **cube number** is the product of a number multiplied by itself 3 times.

Maths Symbols

➕ Addition *(add), plus, sum, total* $4 + 3 = 7$

➖ Subtraction *(subtract), minus, take-away* $7 - 3 = 4$

✖ Multiplication *(multiply), times, product* $3 \times 5 = 15$

➗ Division *(divide), sharing* $15 \div 5 = 3$

---

is Equal to *(the same value)* $\frac{1}{2} = 0.5$

is Approximately Equal to $\frac{1}{3} \approx 0.3$

is Not Equal to *(different value)* $3 \neq 4$

is Equivalent to $5^2 \equiv 25$

< Less than $96 < 124$
96 is less than 124

> Greater than $43 > 27$
43 is greater than 27

≤ Less than or Equal to $x \leq 12$
x is less than or equal to 12

≥ Greater than or Equal to $4 \geq y$
4 is greater than or equal to y

Order of Operations

When calculations involve multiple operations, they must be performed in a specific order.

The acronym **BIDMAS** is used to remember the correct order of operation.

B Brackets	**Brackets** first	$(6 + 2)$
I Indices	Then **indices** or roots	3^2
D Division	Then **divide** or **multiply** in order from left to right	$\dfrac{2 \times 4}{3}$
M Multiplication		
A Addition	Finally, **add** or **subtract** in order from left to right	$3 + 6 - 2$
S Subtraction		

$4 + 2 \times 3$

$2 \times 3 = 6$
$4 + 6 = 10$

B ▶ none
I ▶ none
D or M ▶ $2 \times 3 = 6$
A or S ▶ $4 + 6 = 10$

$20 \div (3 + 2)$

$3 + 2 = 5$
$20 \div 5 = 4$

B ▶ $3 + 2 = 5$
I ▶ none
D or M ▶ $20 \div 5 = 4$
A or S ▶ none

$5 + 3^2 - 6 \times 4$

$3^2 = 9$
$6 \times 4 = 24$
$5 + 9 = 14$
$14 - 24 = -10$

B ▶ none
I ▶ $3^2 = 9$
D or M ▶ $6 \times 4 = 24$
A or S ▶ $5 + 9 = 14$
$14 - 24 = -10$

$6 - 2 + 4 - 3$

$6 - 2 = 4$
$4 + 4 = 8$
$8 - 3 = 5$

B ▶ none
I ▶ none
D or M ▶ none
A or S ▶ $6 - 2 = 4$
$4 + 4 = 8$
$8 - 3 = 5$

$(2^2 + 4)^2 \times 4$

$2^2 = 4$
$4 + 4 = 8$
$8^2 = 64$
$64 \times 4 = 256$

B ▶ $2^2 = 4$
$4 + 4 = 8$
I ▶ $8^2 = 64$
D or M ▶ $64 \times 4 = 256$
A or S ▶ none

Within brackets, order of operations still apply so indices are performed before addition.

$(3 + 8 \div 2)^2$

$8 \div 2 = 4$
$3 + 4 = 7$
$7^2 = 49$

B ▶ $8 \div 2 = 4$
$3 + 4 = 7$
I ▶ $7^2 = 49$
D or M ▶ none
A or S ▶ none

Within brackets, order of operations still apply so division is performed before addition.

8

daydream EDUCATION

Estimating

Sometimes you need to estimate answers to questions. This is often achieved by rounding the numbers in a question to one or two significant figures (s.f.) so that you can perform the calculation in your head.

Example: Estimate the answer to 92 × 8.

1 Round both numbers to the nearest ten.

92 rounded to the nearest ten is 90.
8 rounded to the nearest ten is 10.

2 Perform the calculation.

90 × 10 = 900
The answer is approximately 900.

Real-Life Examples

Poppy is a landscape gardener. She buys 4 bags of gravel at £51.60 each. Approximately how much did Poppy spend on gravel?

1 Round £51.60 to the nearest ten.

51.60 rounded to the nearest ten is 50.

2 Multiply the number of bags (4) by 50 to calculate an estimate for the total cost of the bags of gravel.

4 × 50 = 200
Poppy spent approximately £200 on gravel.

Ricky is a delivery driver. His van has a fuel economy of 60 miles per gallon (mpg). Petrol costs £5.86 per gallon. Last week, Ricky drove 892 miles. Approximately how much did he spend on petrol?

1 Round £5.86 to the nearest whole number (pound).

5.86 rounded to the nearest whole number is 6.

2 Divide 6 by 60 to calculate Ricky's petrol costs per mile.

6 ÷ 60 = 0.10
Cost per mile = £0.10 or 10p

3 Round 892 to the nearest hundred.

892 rounded to the nearest hundred is 900.

4 Multiply the cost per mile by the number of miles travelled to calculate Ricky's total petrol cost.

0.1 × 900 = 90
Ricky spent approximately £90 on petrol.

Practice

1 (a) Greenwood Town's stadium has a capacity of 24,395. If 12,642 people attended the last game, approximately how many empty seats were there?

1 (b) Greenwood's next game is against their local rivals. They have sold 15,429 tickets, and their opponents have sold 3,416 tickets. Approximately how many empty seats will there be at this game?

Addition & Subtraction

Addition +

In addition, two or more numbers are added together to find the total (or sum). The symbol for addition is ⊕

In an assessment, you may not always be directly instructed to add. Therefore, keep an eye out for these key terms:

increase   plus   sum   more   total

Subtraction –

In subtraction, one or more numbers are taken away from another number to find what is left over (the difference). The symbol for subtraction is ⊖

In an assessment, you may not always be directly instructed to subtract. Therefore, keep an eye out for these key terms:

decrease   minus   less   take-away   deduct   left over

Real-Life Example 1

Mason has saved £500 to spend on presents for his family. Everything he wants to buy is listed below. Does he have enough money to buy everything on the list?

Add up the price of all presents:

86 + 34 + 79 + 120 + 20 + 50 + 42 + 19 = £450

Mason has £500 and the total cost of the presents is £450. Therefore, he has enough money to buy the presents.

Mum & Dad	Spa day	£86
	Photobook	£34
	Rugby tickets	£79
Grandad & Grandma	Concert tickets	£120
	Chocolates	£20
Josh	Jeans	£50
Zoe	Perfume	£42
Beth	Toys	£19

daydream
EDUCATION

Olivia is trying to work out her monthly income and expenditure. How much money does Olivia have left over each month after her bills have been paid?

Monthly wage

Income (after tax) £2,100

Step 1 – Add the bills to work out Olivia's total expenditure on bills:

60 + 80 + 320 + 172 + 60 + 120 + 320 = 1,132

Olivia's total expenditure on bills is £1,132

Step 2 – Subtract the total cost of Olivia's bills from her income:

Remember to include the correct unit of measure in your answer.

2,100 – 1,132 = 968

Olivia has £968 left over at the end of each month.

Monthly Bills	
Gas	£60
Electric	£80
Rent	£320
Council Tax	£172
TV, Phone & Internet	£60
Insurances	£120
Food & Toiletries	£320

Olivia pays £560 for repairs to her car and £79 to get her hair coloured. She also wants to buy a new TV, which costs £319. Does she have enough money to buy the TV?

Special Offer
£700   £319

Step 1 – Subtract 560 and 79 from 968:

968 – 560 – 79 = 329

Step 2 - Identify if Olivia has enough money left over to buy the TV.

Money left over = £329   Cost of TV = £319

Olivia has enough money to buy the TV.

Practice

1 There are 18,464 people at Westdale Stadium: 2,243 people in the East Stand, 6,492 in the Bank Stand and 5,430 in the River Stand. How many people are in the remaining stand?

_____

_____

2 Oak School has a year 7 pupil admissions number of 180. The table to the right shows the number of applications the school has received to join year 7 in September. Does the school have enough places?

School	Applications
St John's School	32
Woodlands School	48
Newton School	35
Beacon Primary School	43
Other	24

_____

_____

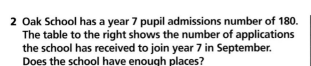

Multiplication

Multiplication is the process of scaling one number by another.

The symbol for multiplication is ⊗

When a multiplication problem involves whole numbers greater than 1, multiplication can be performed through repeated addition:

2 × 4 = 4 lots of 2:   **1** **2** **3** **4**
2 + 2 + 2 + 2 = 8

It doesn't matter which order the factors (2 and 4) are in, the answer is the same:

4 × 2 = 2 lots of 4:   **1** **2**
4 + 4 = 8

In an assessment, you may not always be directly instructed to multiply. Therefore, keep an eye out for these key terms:

multiply   product   **by**   times   **lots of**

Real-Life Example 1

Kamil and five of his friends are selling tickets for a fundraising event at their local community centre. They have each been given 28 tickets.

Kamil and his friends sell all of the tickets. How many tickets have they sold in total?	The tickets cost £4 each. How much money have Kamil and his friends raised?
Multiply the number of tickets sold by each person **by the** number of people (remember to include Kamil):	Multiply the cost of each ticket by the total number of tickets sold.
28 × 6 = 168	**4 × 168 = 672**
Kamil and his friends sold 168 tickets in total.	**Kamil and his friends raised £672.**

daydream EDUCATION

In her job as an electrician, Sophie gets paid every 4 weeks. If she earns £12 per hour and works 8 hours a day, Monday to Friday, how much does she get paid (before tax)?

1	Work out how many hours Sophie works over a 4-week period.	Monday to Friday = 5 days a week 5 days × 8 hours = 40 hours 40 hours = 1 week 4 × 40 hours = 160 hours
2	Multiply the number of hours worked by Sophie's rate of pay.	**160 × 12 = 1,920**

Sophie gets paid £1,920 every 4 weeks.

 Practice

1 Zuri is buying football kits for 15 players in her team. The full kit costs £42. How much will it cost to buy kits for all 15 players?

_____

_____

2 Ellis owns a fruit and veg shop. He has bought five boxes of apples, four boxes of oranges, three boxes of pears and two boxes of lemons. Using the information below, calculate how much stock Ellis has of each fruit.

Fruit	Quantity per box
Apples	104
Oranges	64
Pears	80
Lemons	48

_____

_____

_____

_____

3 Jake is tiling a wall that is 12 m². A pack of tiles covers 3 m² and costs £40. What is the total cost of tiles needed to tile the wall?

_____

_____

_____

_____

Hint: this question involves multiplication and division.

Division

Division is the process of splitting a number or an object into equal parts.

Division ÷

The symbol for division is ÷

When a division problem involves whole numbers greater than 1, division can be performed through repeated subtraction:

$$15 \div 3 = 5: \quad 15 - \underset{1}{3} - \underset{2}{3} - \underset{3}{3} - \underset{4}{3} - \underset{5}{3} = 0$$

To reach zero, 3 is subtracted 5 times from 15. Therefore, 15 divided by 3 is 5.

In an assessment, you may not always be directly instructed to divide. Therefore, keep an eye out for these key terms:

 divide

share

  split

how many times

 goes into

Real-Life Example 1

1

Joseph is in charge of organising catering staff for an event hosting 120 people. He needs to ensure that there is one server to every 8 guests. How many servers does he need for the event?

Divide the total number of guests by the number of guests per server:

$$120 \div 8 = 15$$

Joseph needs 15 servers for the event.

2

Elouise is in charge of the buffet for the event. She needs to make 80 portions of lasagne. If one lasagne can be cut into 16 portions, how many lasagnes does Elouise need to make for the event?

Divide the required number of portions by the number of servings in each lasagne:

$$80 \div 16 = 5$$

Elouise needs to make 5 lasagnes.

daydream
EDUCATION

Real-Life Example 2 (includes multiplication and division skills)

Connor owns a café. To make 50 sandwiches he needs 400 grams of butter. Connor is hosting a party at his café, for which he needs 500 sandwiches. If butter comes in 1.5 kilogram tubs, how many tubs of butter will Connor need to buy?

1 Firstly, make the units of measure the same by converting 400 grams into kilograms.

$$1,000 \text{ g} = 1 \text{ kg}$$
$$400 \div 1,000 = 0.4$$
$$400 \text{ g} = 0.4 \text{ kg}$$

2 Calculate how much butter is needed per sandwich by dividing the amount of butter used by the number of sandwiches made.

$$0.4 \div 50 = 0.008$$

3 Now that you know how much butter is needed to make one sandwich, you can calculate how much butter Connor needs to make 500 sandwiches by multiplying the amount of butter needed per sandwich (0.008) by 500.

$$0.008 \times 500 = 4$$
Connor needs 4 kilos of butter to make 500 sandwiches.

4 To calculate how many tubs of butter Connor needs to buy, divide 4 kilos by 1.5.

$$4 \div 1.5 = 2.6$$

Connor needs 2.6 tubs of butter. As he can only buy whole tubs, he will need to buy 3 tubs of butter because 2 tubs will not be enough.

Practice

1 Maddison is a florist. The table below shows the quantities of flowers that she has in stock. She needs to make 23 identical bunches of flowers for a wedding. How many of each flower can she put in each bunch?

Flower	Quantity	Quantity per bunch
White rose	92	
Purple freesia	115	
Green pistache	276	
Lilies	138	

2 Leo is packing an order of books for a school. The dimensions of the boxes and the books are shown below. How many books can he pack into each box?

Box
52 cm
30 cm
75 cm

Book
16 cm
5 cm
24 cm

Hint: this question involves multiplication and division.

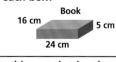

Negative Numbers

A negative number is any number that is less than zero. Negative numbers are denoted by a minus sign: **–**.

The number line below shows the integers, or whole numbers, from -10 to 10.

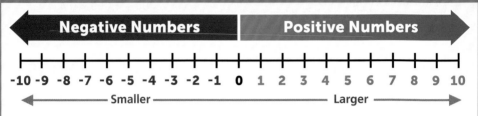

Negative Numbers | **Positive Numbers**

-10 -9 -8 -7 -6 -5 -4 -3 -2 -1 0 1 2 3 4 5 6 7 8 9 10

← Smaller ———————————— Larger →

Numbers to the **left** on a number line are smaller than those to their **right**. The value of negative numbers decreases from right to left. For example, –7 is less than –2.

Real-life examples of negative numbers include:

Temperature | **Bank Balances**

The following rules apply when adding or subtracting negative numbers.

Adding a negative number is the same as subtracting. It produces a lower value.

$$2 \boxed{+ -3} = -1$$

+ –3

-2   -1   0   1   2   3

If you **add a** negative number, you move to the **left** on a number line.

Subtracting a negative number is the same as adding. It produces a higher value.

$$4 \boxed{- -2} = 6$$

– –2

3   4   5   6   7   8

If you **subtract a** negative number, you move to the **right** on a number line.

The following rules apply when multiplying or dividing negative numbers.

$$2 \times -3 = -6$$

Multiplying a positive number by a negative number (and vice versa) produces a negative number.

$$21 \div -3 = -7$$

Dividing a positive number by a negative number (and vice versa) produces a negative number.

$$-2 \times -3 = 6$$

Multiplying two negative numbers produces a positive number.

$$-18 \div -3 = 6$$

Dividing a negative number by a negative number produces a positive number.

---

daydream EDUCATION

Callum has –£452 in his bank account.

He pays £325 into the account. What is his new balance?	Later that day, Callum spends £155 on new clothes. What is his new balance?
Add the deposited amount to the bank balance:	Subtract the amount Callum spent from the bank balance:
$-452 + 325 = -127$	$-127 - 155 = -282$
Callum's new bank account balance is –£127.	Callum's new bank account balance is –£282.

Real-Life Example 2

The temperature in Toronto is –7°C. The temperature in Bristol is 5°C.

What is the difference in temperature between Toronto and Bristol?	The next day, the temperature in Bristol dropped by 8°C. What was the temperature?
Using a number line, count up from –7 up to 5.	Using a number line, count down 8 from 5°C.

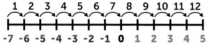

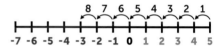

The difference in temperature is 12°C.

The temperature in Bristol was –3°C.

Without a number line, subtract the temperature in Toronto from the temperature in Bristol.	Without a number line, subtract 8 from 5°C.
$5 \boxed{- -7} = 12$	$5 - 8 = -3$

Subtracting a negative number is the same as adding.

Practice

1 The temperature in London is 4°C. It is 12 degrees colder in Moscow. What is the temperature in Moscow?

2 A summary of Ella's Beauty Salon's accounts is shown below. Complete the balances for September and December.

Month	July	Aug	Sep	Oct	Nov	Dec
Total Deposits	-	£2,690	£1,300	£2,300	–£2,100	£1,090
Balance	–£5,000	–£2,310		£1,290	–£810	

Number Lines & Scales

Number lines and scales can help in a wide variety of maths problems, whether it be adding, subtracting, ordering or comparing numbers.

Reading Number Lines and Scales

Number Lines

Each small line on the number line is worth 2, so the arrow is pointing at 26.

Each small line on the number line is worth 0.25, so the arrow is pointing at 1.75.

Thermometer

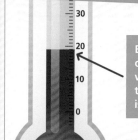

Each small line on the scale is worth 1°C, so the temperature is 19°C.

Each small line on the scale is worth 2°C, so the temperature is –6°C.

Weighing Scales

Each small line on the scale is worth 25 kg, so the item weighs 175 kg.

Each small line on the scale is worth 20 g, so the item weighs 640 g.

daydream EDUCATION

If you are unable to identify the unknown values on a scale, follow the steps outlined below.

How much water is in this jug?

1 Identify the difference between the known values on the scale. The difference between 1000 and 2000 is 1000:

$$2000 - 1000 = 1000$$

2 Identify how many segments there are between the known values. There are 4 segments between the known values.

3 Divide the difference between the known values by the number of segments: $1000 \div 4 = 250$

4 Each increment on the scale is worth 250 ml, so there are 1750 ml of water in the jug.

Real-Life Example

Harvey is an apprentice chef. His head chef has asked him to weigh 120 g of flour. Look at the scales below. Identify the point on the scale that represents 120 g.

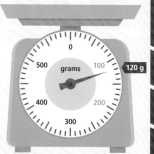

1 Identify the difference between the known values on the scale:

$$200 - 100 = 100$$

2 Identify how many segments there are between the known values. There are 10 segments between the known values.

3 Divide the difference between the known values by the number of segments: $100 \div 10 = 10$

4 Each increment on the scale is worth 10 g, so the second line after the 100 line represents 120 grams.

Practice

1 How much water is in the measuring jug?

2 What is the temperature according to the thermometer?

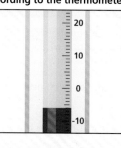

3 How much does the bag of sugar weigh?

Fractions

When a whole or group is divided into equal parts a fraction is created.

The top number is called the **numerator**.

It represents the number of parts being considered.

$$\frac{1}{2}$$

The bottom number is called the **denominator**.

It represents the total number of parts.

When the denominator and numerator are equal, the fraction is equal to 1.

Parts of a Whole

The cake has been cut into three equal pieces. Each piece is one-third.

One-third ($\frac{1}{3}$) has been eaten.

Two-thirds ($\frac{2}{3}$) are left.

The box has been split into eight equal compartments. Each compartment is one-eighth.

Three-eighths ($\frac{3}{8}$) are full.

Five-eighths ($\frac{5}{8}$) are empty.

Parts of a Group

There are four paint cans.

One-quarter ($\frac{1}{4}$) is blue.

Three-quarters ($\frac{3}{4}$) are yellow.

There are five students in the team.

Two-fifths ($\frac{2}{5}$) are boys.

Three-fifths ($\frac{3}{5}$) are girls.

Practice

1 Olly has cut an MDF sheet into ten equally-sized pieces. He has used seven pieces. What fraction of the sheet is left?

2 (a) What fraction of the shampoo has been used?

2 (b) If another $\frac{2}{5}$ is used, what fraction of the bottle will be left?

daydream
EDUCATION

Finding a Fraction of an Amount

To find a fraction of an amount, divide the amount by the bottom number (denominator) and then multiply the answer by the top number (numerator).

	What is $\frac{3}{5}$ of 750?	What is $\frac{1}{4}$ of 200?	What is $\frac{3}{7}$ of 126?
Divide the amount by the denominator.	$750 \div 5 = 150$	$200 \div 4 = 50$	$126 \div 7 = 18$
Multiply the answer by the numerator.	$150 \times 3 = 450$	$50 \times 1 = 50$	$18 \times 3 = 54$

Real-Life Example

Grace earns £1,950 a month (after tax). She spends two-fifths of this on her mortgage.

How much is Grace's mortgage?

Divide Grace's wage (the amount) by the denominator:	$1950 \div 5 = 390$
Multiply the answer by the numerator.	$390 \times 2 = 780$

Grace's mortgage is £780 a month.

Grace uses the train to commute to and from work. The train operator is offering one-third off its monthly season ticket, which costs £990. What is the sale price of the ticket?

Divide the price of the ticket by the denominator.	$990 \div 3 = 330$
Multiply the answer by the numerator.	$330 \times 1 = 330$
Subtract the discount from the normal price.	$990 - 330 = 660$

The sale price of the season ticket is £660.

Practice

1 (a) Aston is a plumber. He has a trade account at his local hardware store. Complete the table below to calculate Aston's bill for his latest order.

Product	Quantity	Price	Total	Trade Discount	Discount	Price
Radiator	3	£79		$\frac{1}{4}$		
Pipes	1	£26		$\frac{3}{10}$		
Pipe fittings	1	£48		$\frac{3}{10}$		
					Total	

1 (b) After every job, Aston asks his customers to complete a survey. Out of his last 54 jobs, five-sixths of customers have rated him as excellent. How many people rated him as excellent?

Equivalent Fractions

Equivalent fractions are equal. They have different numerators and denominators but are equal in value. You can make equivalent fractions by multiplying or dividing both the numerator and denominator by the same number.

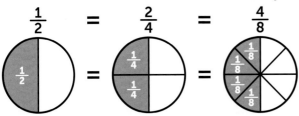

Look how these fractions take up the same amount of each circle but the numerators and denominators are different.

A fraction wall can be used to help identify equivalent fractions.

$$\frac{1}{2} = \frac{4}{8} \qquad \frac{1}{3} = \frac{2}{6}$$

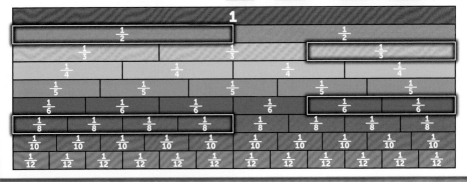

Which of the following fractions are equal?

$$\frac{1}{2} \qquad \frac{3}{15} \qquad \frac{4}{8} \qquad \frac{6}{9} \qquad \frac{1}{5} \qquad \frac{2}{3}$$

Simplifying Fractions

To simplify a fraction, the **numerator** and **denominator** must be divided by their **highest common factor** (the largest whole number that is a factor of both numbers) to create **like fractions**.

$$\frac{10}{15} \rightarrow$$

Factors of 10: 1, 2, 5, 10

Factors of 15: 1, 3, 5, 15

5 is the largest factor of both 10 and 15 so:

$$\frac{10}{15} \xrightarrow{\div 5}{\div 5} = \frac{2}{3}$$

Simplifying in Steps

Sometimes it is easier to simplify in steps. Divide the top and bottom numbers of the fraction by a common factor until they cannot be divided any further.

$$\frac{60}{100} \xrightarrow{\div 10}{\div 10} = \frac{6}{10} \xrightarrow{\div 2}{\div 2} = \frac{3}{5}$$

daydream EDUCATION

1 Leah is the manager of a hotel. 32 out of the 40 rooms in the hotel are booked for Saturday night. What fraction of the rooms are booked? Give your answer in its simplest form.

| Write 32 out of 40 as a fraction. | $$\frac{32}{40}$$ |

| Identify the factors of both numbers, and then identify their highest common factor. | Factors of 32: 1, 2, 4, 8, 16, 32
 Factors of 40: 1, 2, 4, 5, 8, 10, 20, 40 |

| Divide the numerator and the denominator by their HCF. | $$\frac{32}{40} \begin{array}{c} \div 8 \\ = \\ \div 8 \end{array} \frac{4}{5}$$ |

Four-fifths ($\frac{4}{5}$) of the rooms in the hotel have been booked.

2 To achieve her target for the month, Leah needs eight-tenths of the rooms to be booked on Sunday night. 28 rooms are currently booked. Has Leah hit her target?

| Write 28 out of 40 as a fraction. | $$\frac{28}{40}$$ |

| Identify the factors of both numbers, and then identify their highest common factor. | Factors of 28: 1, 2, 4, 7, 14, 28
 Factors of 40: 1, 2, 4, 5, 8, 10, 20, 40 |

| Divide the numerator and the denominator by their HCF. | $$\frac{28}{40} \begin{array}{c} \div 4 \\ = \\ \div 4 \end{array} \frac{7}{10}$$ |

Only seven-tenths ($\frac{7}{10}$) of the rooms in the hotel have been booked, so Leah has not achieved her target.

Practice

1 (a) George is a delivery driver. By 10 o'clock, he had delivered 12 out of his 72 parcels. Write this as a fraction in its simplest form.

1 (b) By 11 o'clock, George had delivered 28 parcels. Write this as a fraction in its simplest form.

1 (c) What fraction of parcels does George still need to deliver?

Adding & Subtracting Fractions

To add or subtract fractions, their **denominators** must be the same. Fractions with the same denominator are known as **like fractions**.

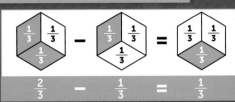

$$\frac{1}{4} + \frac{2}{4} = \frac{3}{4}$$

$$\frac{2}{3} - \frac{1}{3} = \frac{1}{3}$$

Real-Life Example

Sarah and Luca ordered a pizza. Sarah ate $\frac{5}{8}$ and Luca ate $\frac{1}{8}$. How much of the pizza is left?

$$\frac{5}{8} + \frac{1}{8} = \frac{6}{8}$$

$\frac{6}{8}$ or $\frac{3}{4}$ of the pizza has been eaten so $\frac{2}{8}$ or $\frac{1}{4}$ of the pizza is left.

When the denominators are different (known as unlike fractions), multiply one or both fractions so they share the same denominator before performing the addition or subtraction. To do this, identify the lowest common multiple of each denominator.

What is $\frac{1}{4} + \frac{1}{3}$?

1	Identify the lowest common multiple of the denominators in the fractions.	Multiples of 4: 4, 8, 12, 16 $\quad \frac{1}{4} + \frac{1}{3} \quad$ Multiples of 3: 3, 6, 9, 12, 15, 18
2	Multiply each fraction by the appropriate number so they share the lowest common denominator of 12.	$\frac{1}{4} \begin{smallmatrix} \times 3 \\ = \\ \times 3 \end{smallmatrix} \frac{3}{12}$ $\qquad$ $\frac{1}{3} \begin{smallmatrix} \times 4 \\ = \\ \times 4 \end{smallmatrix} \frac{4}{12}$
3	Add the fractions together.	$\frac{3}{12} + \frac{4}{12} = \frac{7}{12}$

Real-Life Example

Lewis has $\frac{2}{3}$ of a bag of cement. How much cement will he have left if he uses another $\frac{1}{6}$?

1	Identify the lowest common multiple of the denominators in the fractions.	Multiples of 3: 3, 6, 9 $\quad \frac{2}{3} - \frac{1}{6} \quad$ Multiples of 6: 6, 12, 18
2	Multiply each fraction by the appropriate number so they share the lowest common denominator of 6.	$\frac{2}{3} \begin{smallmatrix} \times 2 \\ = \\ \times 2 \end{smallmatrix} \frac{4}{6}$ $\qquad$ $\frac{1}{6} \begin{smallmatrix} \times 1 \\ = \\ \times 1 \end{smallmatrix} \frac{1}{6}$
3	Subtract $\frac{1}{6}$ from $\frac{4}{6}$.	$\frac{4}{6} - \frac{1}{6} = \frac{3}{6} = \frac{1}{2}$ $\qquad$ Lewis has $\frac{1}{2}$ a bag of cement left.

daydream
EDUCATION

$\frac{2}{5} + \frac{3}{4}$ | $\frac{2}{5} = 2 \div 5 = 0.4$ | $\frac{1}{4} = 1 \div 4 = 0.25$ | $0.4 + 0.25 = 0.65$

Real-Life Examples

Emily, Mohammad and Mark are doing a charity relay run. So far, Emily has run $\frac{1}{8}$ of the distance, Mohammad has run $\frac{1}{4}$ of the distance and Mark has run $\frac{3}{10}$ of the distance. How much of the run have they completed?

1	Convert the fractions to decimals.	Emily: $1 \div 8 = 0.125$ Mohammad: $1 \div 4 = 0.25$ Mark: $3 \div 10 = 0.3$
2	Add the decimal answers together.	$0.125 + 0.25 + 0.3 = 0.675$

They have completed 0.675, $\frac{67.5}{100}$ or 67.5% of the race.

Jodie, Dean and Paul have been renovating a house. Jodie did $\frac{2}{5}$ of the work and Dean did $\frac{1}{2}$ of the work. How much of the work did Paul do?

1	Convert the fractions to decimals.	Jodie: $2 \div 5 = 0.4$ Dean: $1 \div 2 = 0.5$
2	Add Jodie's and Dean's totals together, and then subtract them from 1 (the total) to calculate Paul's work contribution.	$0.4 + 0.5 = 0.9$ $1 - 0.9 = 0.1$

Paul did 0.1, $\frac{1}{10}$ or 10% of the work.

Practice

1 Mollie and Ravi are packing orders. Mollie has packed $\frac{1}{4}$ of the orders and Ravi has packed $\frac{3}{5}$ of the orders. What fraction of the orders have been packed?

_____

2 Isla owns a car-washing business. To save money, she buys car shampoo in huge containers. The amount of the car shampoo container she has used this week is shown below.

Mon	Tues	Wed	Thurs	Fri	Sat	Sun
-	-	$\frac{1}{10}$	$\frac{1}{8}$	$\frac{1}{5}$	$\frac{2}{5}$	$\frac{1}{8}$

How much of the container of car shampoo has Isla used? Give your answer as a decimal, fraction or percentage.

_____

_____

_____

Mixed Numbers & Improper Fractions

Mixed numbers and improper fractions are two different ways of writing fractions that are greater than one, or a whole.

The fraction below can be written as a mixed number or as an improper fraction.

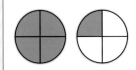

$=$

Mixed Numbers contain a whole number and a fractional part.

$1\frac{1}{4}$

$=$

Improper Fractions have a numerator that is greater than or equal to the denominator.

$\frac{5}{4}$

Converting Improper Fractions to Mixed Numbers

Divide the **numerator** by the **denominator**.

$\frac{9}{4}$

4 goes into **9** twice with **1** left over, therefore:

$9 \div 4 = 2$ remainder 1

You now have 2 wholes (ones) and 1 remainder, which becomes the numerator.

$2\frac{1}{4}$

The **denominator** does not change.

Therefore:

$\frac{9}{4} = 2\frac{1}{4}$

A visual representation of the conversion is shown below.

Converting Mixed Numbers to Improper Fractions

Multiply the **denominator** by the whole number.

$3\frac{1}{2}$

$2 \times 3 = 6$

Add this number to the **numerator**.

$6 + 1 = 7$

This creates:

$\frac{7}{2}$

Therefore:

$3\frac{1}{2} = \frac{7}{2}$

A visual representation of the conversion is shown below.

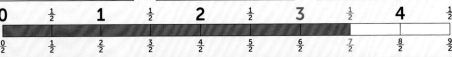

Complete the following conversions: $\frac{8}{3} =$ _____ $8\frac{2}{3} =$ _____ $\frac{34}{8} =$ _____ $4\frac{1}{7} =$ _____

daydream EDUCATION

When performing calculations involving mixed numbers and improper fractions, it is often easier to convert them to decimals and then perform the calculations.

$$3\frac{2}{5} = 2 \div 5 + 3 = 3.4$$

$$\frac{10}{4} = 10 \div 4 = 2.5$$

Real-Life Examples

Olivia, Liam and Jake have been picking strawberries. Olivia has $2\frac{1}{2}$ baskets, Liam has $3\frac{1}{4}$ baskets and Jake has $3\frac{3}{4}$ baskets. How many baskets do they have in total?

1	Convert the mixed numbers to decimals.	Olivia: $1 \div 2 + 2 = 2.5$ Liam: $1 \div 4 + 3 = 3.25$ Jake: $3 \div 4 + 3 = 3.75$
2	Add the decimals together.	$2.5 + 3.25 + 3.75 = 9.5$

They have 9.5 or $9\frac{1}{2}$ baskets of strawberries in total.

Vicki runs a photo-framing business. She needs to send 8 small frames, which weigh $2\frac{3}{4}$ kilograms each, to a customer but the maximum weight allowance for a parcel is 23 kg. Can Vicki send all the frames together in one parcel?

1	Convert the mixed number to a decimal.	$3 \div 4 + 2 = 2.75$
2	Multiply the decimal by the total number of parcels to calculate the total weight.	$2.75 \times 8 = 22$ kg

Vicki can send the frames in one parcel, as 8 frames weigh less than 23 kg.

Practice

1 Isabelle is a landscape gardener. She has $8\frac{1}{2}$ tonnes of top soil that she needs to split into five evenly-sized polybags. How much top soil does she need to put in each bag?

_____

_____

2 Lee is going to visit his friend Maria in Barcelona. A breakdown of his journey is shown below.

$\frac{3}{4}$ hour	$2\frac{1}{4}$ hours	$1\frac{1}{2}$ hours

Lee's Home —— Heathrow Airport —— Barcelona Airport —— Maria's House

How long did the journey take in total?

_____

_____

Place Value

The value of each digit in a number depends upon its position, or place. The position or place of each digit represents a power of ten.

Thousands 1000s	Hundreds 100s	Tens 10s	Ones 1s	Decimal Point	Tenths 1/10	Hundredths 1/100	Thousandths 1/1000
1	6	8	2	.	4	7	3
Whole numbers with a value of 0 or more					Numbers with a value of less than 1		

Look at what each digit in the numbers below represents.

324
is made up of:
3 hundreds
2 tens
4 ones

46
is made up of:
4 tens
6 ones

6457
is made up of:
6 thousands
4 hundreds
5 tens
7 ones

2.45
is made up of:
2 ones
4 tenths
5 hundredths

Look at the numbers below. What does the digit 4 in each number represent? Can you put the numbers in order from smallest to largest?

34   426   748   8421   304   3.04   7.46

Multiplying and Dividing by Powers of 10

The value of a digit in a number changes when its place in the number changes.

Each digit to the left is ten times the value of the same digit to its right. Therefore, when a number is multiplied by 10, all digits in the number become ten times bigger.

Each digit to the right is one-tenth the value of the same digit to its left. Therefore, when a number is divided by 10, all digits in the number become ten times smaller.

8.73 × 10 = 87.3

Notice how all numbers have moved one place to the left.

97.8 ÷ 10 = 9.78

Notice how all numbers have moved one place to the right.

daydream EDUCATION

Decimal Calculations

Decimal calculations involving addition, subtraction, multiplication and division can be performed on a calculator in the same way as whole-number calculations.

Addition & Subtraction

Chloe is a freelance graphic designer. She has agreed a new 21-hour project with a client. The hours she has worked so far are shown below. How many hours has she got left?

Mon	Tue	Wed	Thur	Fri
5.5 hrs	2.25 hrs	3 hrs	4.75 hrs	1.25 hrs

1. Add together the number of hours worked so far: 5.5 + 2.25 + 3 + 4.75 + 1.25 = 16.75

2. Subtract Chloe's total hours worked from the project total: 21 – 16.75 = 4.25

Chloe has 4.25 hours left to work on the project.

Multiplication

Chloe agreed a rate of £30.50 an hour with her client. How much will Chloe get paid for the project?

Multiply Chloe's rate by the number of hours in the project:

£30.50 × 21 = £640.50

Division

Chloe worked 32.5 hours on a previous project. Because it was a larger block of work, she charged a lower rate. She got paid a total of £916.50. What was her hourly rate?

Divide Chloe's total pay by the number of hours she worked:

£916.50 ÷ 32.5 = £28.20

Practice

1 (a) Nikita is a sales rep for an IT company. She has just sold a suite of 20 tablets to a customer at a price of £229.79 each. What is the total price of the suite of tablets?

1 (b) Nikita has agreed to supply her customer with 20 tablet cases at a reduced price of £272.80. What is the unit price of each case?

1 (c) What is the total price of the order?

1 (d) Nikita is working out her mileage as part of her expenses claim. Her mileage for each day last week is shown below. How many miles did she drive last week in total?

Mon	Tue	Wed	Thur	Fri	Total
81.8	91.4	219.4	32.7	102.3	

1 (e) Nikita has calculated that 61.4 miles were for personal use. She needs to deduct this from her expenses claim. How many miles will Nikita be claiming for?

Comparing & Ordering Decimals

Digits to the right of the decimal point are known as decimals and have a value of less than one.

Comparing and Ordering Decimal Numbers

To compare and order decimal numbers, you need to compare place values digit by digit.

| 6.34 | 0.69 | 3.09 | 0.64 | 10.2 |

To order the numbers above in order of size:

1 Put the numbers in a place value table and fill any blanks with zeros.

Tens	Ones	.	Tenths	Hundredths
0	6	.	3	4
0	0	.	6	9
0	3	.	0	9
0	0	.	6	4
1	0	.	2	0

2 Identify the largest number in the column that is farthest to the left.

There is only one number that has a digit in the tens column; 10.20. Therefore, 10.20 is the largest number.

Tens	Ones	.	Tenths	Hundredths
0	6	.	3	4
0	0	.	6	9
0	3	.	0	9
0	0	.	6	4
1	0	.	2	0

3 Move to the next column to the right and compare the numbers.

Six is the largest number in the ones column. Therefore, 6.34 is the next largest number, followed by 3.09.

Tens	Ones	.	Tenths	Hundredths
0	6	.	3	4
0	0	.	6	9
0	3	.	0	9
0	0	.	6	4
1	0	.	2	0

4 Move to the next column to the right and compare the numbers.

Both numbers in this column are the same; 6.

If both numbers are the same, compare the numbers in the next column to the right.

9 is larger than 4, so 0.69 is larger than 0.64.

Tens	Ones	.	Tenths	Hundredths
0	6	.	3	4
0	0	.	6	9
0	3	.	0	9
0	0	.	6	4
1	0	.	2	0

The order from smallest to largest is: 0.64, 0.69, 3.09, 6.34, 10.2

daydream
EDUCATION

Natalie is helping with the long jump trials at her local athletics club.
Help her to order the distances below from shortest to longest.

| 6.308 m | 6.217 m | 6.935 m | 5.61 m | 5.609 m |

1 Put the numbers in a place value table and fill any blanks with zeros.

Ones	.	Tenths	Hundredths	Thousandths
6	.	3	0	8
6	.	2	1	7
6	.	9	3	5
5	.	6	1	0
5	.	6	0	9

Identify the largest number in the column that is farthest to the left.

2 There are three numbers with the same value; 6. If there are numbers with the same value, compare the numbers in the next column to the right.

9 is the largest digit in the tenths column so 6.935 is the largest number, followed by 6.308, then 6.217 because three is larger than two.

Ones	.	Tenths	Hundredths	Thousandths
6	.	3	0	8
6	.	2	1	7
6	.	9	3	5
5	.	6	1	0
5	.	6	0	9

Compare the numbers in the tenths column for the remaining measurements.

3 Both numbers are the same; 6.

If both numbers are the same, compare the numbers in the next column to the right.

1 is larger than 0, so 5.610 is larger than 5.609.

Ones	.	Tenths	Hundredths	Thousandths
6	.	3	0	8
6	.	2	1	7
6	.	9	3	5
5	.	6	1	0
5	.	6	0	9

The order from shortest to longest is: 5.609 m, 5.61 m, 6.217 m, 6.308 m, 6.935 m

Practice

1 Natalie's friend, Ashley, is helping to record the 100 m times at the same competition. Help him to order the times from fastest to slowest:

| 11.024 | 10.807 | 11.9 | 11.26 | 11.49 |

The order from fastest to slowest is:

Rounding Numbers

It is not always necessary to use exact numbers, so rounding is used to provide simpler numbers that are easier to use.

Rounding Using a Number Line

Number lines are used to help determine whether to round a number up or down.

Is it nearer 600 or 700?

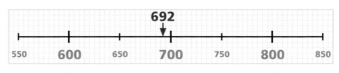

692

| 550 | 600 | 650 | 700 | 750 | 800 | 850 |

692 rounded to the nearest hundred is 700.
The number line shows that **692** is closer to **700** than it is to **600**.

The same rule applies when rounding to decimal places.

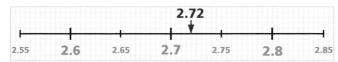

2.72

| 2.55 | 2.6 | 2.65 | 2.7 | 2.75 | 2.8 | 2.85 |

Is it nearer 2.7 or 2.8?

2.72 rounded to one decimal place is 2.7.
The number line shows that **2.72** is closer to **2.7** than it is to **2.8**.
When rounding numbers to decimal places, only consider the digits **after** the decimal point.

Rounding Without a Number Line

Without a number line, look at the first digit to the right of the digit you are rounding.

If the number is less than 5, leave it alone.

To round 1,734 to the nearest hundred…

Identify the digit in the hundreds' place.

↓

1,734

Look at the number to the right of the hundreds' digit.

1,734

Less than 5 – leave it alone.

Therefore, 1,734 rounded to the nearest hundred is 1,700.

If the number is 5 or more, round up.

To round 8.3643 to the nearest tenth…

Identify the digit in the tenths' place.

↓

8.3643

Look at the number to the right of the tenths' digit.

8.3643

5 or more – round up.

Therefore, 8.3643 rounded to the nearest tenth is 8.4.

daydream
EDUCATION

Ella is training for a 10 km fun run. The table below shows the distances she has run over the last 5 days. Round Ella's distances to the nearest kilometre.

1 Identify which digit you need to round to.

	Mon	Tue	Wed	Thurs	Fri
	5.73 km	4.29 km	10.31 km	-	8.54 km

2 Look at the first digit to the right of the digit you are rounding. If it is less than 5, leave it alone. If it is 5 or more, round it up.

	Mon	Tue	Wed	Thurs	Fri
	5.73 km	4.29 km	10.31 km	-	8.54 km
	5 or more – round it up	Less than 5 – leave it alone	Less than 5 – leave it alone		5 or more – round it up

3 Ella's distances rounded to the nearest kilometre are as follows:

	Mon	Tue	Wed	Thurs	Fri
	6 km	4 km	10 km	-	9 km

Practice

1 Round the populations below to the specified degree of accuracy.

Country	Population	Round to nearest	Rounded Population
Norway	5,254,694	million	
Iceland	332,474	hundred	
Denmark	5,711,870	thousand	
Sweden	9,837,533	million	
Finland	5,503,132	hundred	

2 Mia is a mobile hairdresser. Her costs for the month are listed below. She wants a rough idea of her total costs, so she can ensure she has enough money in her bank account. Round the costs to the nearest pound and calculate her total costs.

Item	Cost	Rounded Costs
Hairspray	£18.74	
Shampoo & conditioner	£56.13	
Hair dye	£149.75	
Foil and meche	£35.39	
Fuel	£199.61	

Approximate total cost:

Percentages

The word percent comes from the Latin words *per* and *cent* meaning 'out of every 100'. The symbol for percent is %.

 **1%**

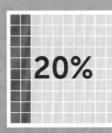 **20%**

 **50%**

 **100%**

Finding a Percentage

What is 20% of 40?

1	Convert the percentage to a decimal.	$20\% = 20 \div 100 = 0.2$
2	Multiply the amount by the decimal.	$40 \times 0.2 = 8$

20% of 40 is 8.

Real-Life Examples

Mitchell wants to buy a house that costs £180,000 but he's not sure if he can afford the 15% deposit. He has £20,000. Does he have enough money for the deposit?

1	Convert the percentage to a decimal: $15 \div 100 = 0.15$
2	Multiply the house price by the decimal: $180{,}000 \times 0.15 = 27{,}000$

15% of £180,000 is £27,000, so Mitchell does not have enough money for the deposit.

Jin is a sports massage therapist. To attract new clients, he is offering a 20% discount on his £30 sessions. What is the discounted price?

1	Convert the percentage to a decimal: $20 \div 100 = 0.2$
2	Multiply Jin's normal price by the decimal: $30 \times 0.2 = 6$

£6 is the discount, not the discounted price. To calculate the discounted price, subtract the discount from the normal price: $30 - 6 = 24$. Jin's discounted price is £24.

Practice

1 (a) Sofia is selling tickets for a music concert. She earns 12% commission on all sales. Last month, she sold 220 tickets at £50 each. How much commission did Sofia earn?

1 (b) There are a total of 8,550 tickets available for the concert. 72% of the tickets have been sold. Calculate the total value of ticket sales based on each ticket being sold at £50.

daydream EDUCATION

Expressing One Quantity as a Percentage of Another

Percentages are used to express how large or small one amount is relative to another amount. For example, percentages are often used to express exam results.

Harry scored 42 out of 56 in his maths exam. He needs 70% to pass. Has Harry passed?

1. Divide Harry's score by the total.	2. Multiply the answer by 100.	Harry scored 75% in his maths exam, so he passed.
$42 \div 56 = 0.75$	$0.75 \times 100 = 75\%$	

A hotel has 66 of its 75 rooms booked for Saturday night. Express this as a percentage.

1. Divide the number of rooms booked by the total number of rooms.	2. Multiply the answer by 100.	88% of the rooms in the hotel have been booked.
$66 \div 75 = 0.88$	$0.88 \times 100 = 88\%$	

Erin is driving 204 miles from Cardiff to Sheffield. She has travelled 82 miles. How far has Erin travelled as a percentage of the total distance?

1. Divide the distance travelled by the total distance.	2. Multiply the answer by 100.	Erin has travelled 40% of the total distance from Cardiff to Sheffield.
$82 \div 204 = 0.40$	$0.40 \times 100 = 40\%$	

Practice

1 Express 24 as a percentage of 30.

2 Roger is a driving instructor. 23 of his 28 lessons for the week have been booked. He always like to have 80% of his lessons filled. Has he achieved this?

3 Harry's burger chain has 560 reviews on Restaurant Rater. Calculate the percentage values for each star rating.

Star Rating	Reviews	Percentage
5 stars	280	
4 stars	140	
3 stars	84	
2 stars	42	
1 stars	14	

Percentage Change

Percentage Increase

Find the value of the percentage and **add** it to the original amount.

Repairs to Charlie's car cost £250 + VAT (20%). What is the cost including VAT?

1 Calculate 20%.
$$250 \times 0.2 = 50$$

2 Add it to the original amount.
$$250 + 50 = 300$$

The total cost of the repairs is £300.

Percentage Decrease

Find the value of the percentage and subtract it from the original amount.

A £40 dress has 10% off in the sale. What is the sale price of the dress?

1 Calculate 10%.
$$40 \times 0.10 = 4$$

2 Subtract it from the original amount.
$$40 - 4 = 36$$

The sale price of the dress is £36.

Percentage Change

$$\text{Percentage change} = \frac{\text{Change in value}}{\text{Original value}} \times 100$$

Last year, Sienna had £3,200 in her bank account. She now has £3,360 despite not having paid in any money.

Calculate the rate of interest on her account.

1 Calculate the change in value (balance).
$$3,360 - 3,200 = 160$$

2 Divide the change in balance by the original balance.
$$160 \div 3,200 = 0.05$$

3 Multiply by 100.
$$0.05 \times 100 = 5$$

The rate of interest on Sienna's account was 5%.

Practice

1. Woodland's Water Park is launching a new water ride. As a result, it is expecting a 15% increase in its visitor numbers this year. Last year there were 184,000 visitors. How many visitors are they expecting this year?

2. Li Na bought a car for £9,495. Over the last 12 months, the car has depreciated in value by 22%. What is the car worth now?

3. Last year, Ryan's car servicing and MOT garage made a profit of £18,000. This year, it made a profit of £23,400. Calculate the business's percentage increase in profit.

daydream EDUCATION

Fractions, Decimals, Percentages

Fractions, decimals and percentages are three different ways of expressing a proportion of a whole.

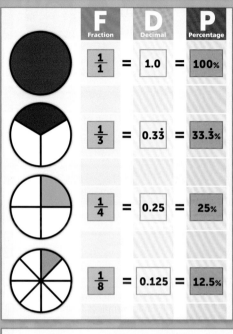

F Fraction	**D** Decimal	**P** Percentage
$\frac{1}{1}$ =	1.0 =	100%
$\frac{1}{3}$ =	0.3̇3 =	33.3̇%
$\frac{1}{4}$ =	0.25 =	25%
$\frac{1}{8}$ =	0.125 =	12.5%

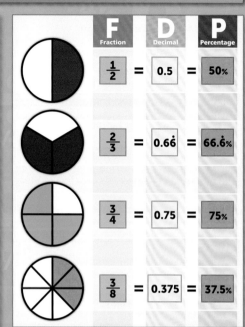

F Fraction	**D** Decimal	**P** Percentage
$\frac{1}{2}$ =	0.5 =	50%
$\frac{2}{3}$ =	0.6̇6 =	66.6̇%
$\frac{3}{4}$ =	0.75 =	75%
$\frac{3}{8}$ =	0.375 =	37.5%

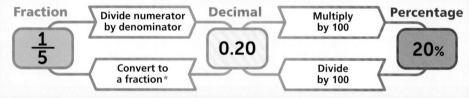

Fraction $\frac{1}{5}$ — Divide numerator by denominator → **Decimal** 0.20 — Multiply by 100 → **Percentage** 20%

Convert to a fraction* ← Divide by 100

* To convert a decimal to a fraction:

1 Multiply the **decimal** by the appropriate power of 10 so it becomes a whole number and use this as the **numerator**.	**2** The power of 10 that the decimal was multiplied by is used as the **denominator**.	**3** Simplify if possible.
0.25 × 100 = 25	$\frac{25}{100}$	$\frac{25}{100}$ → $\frac{÷25}{÷25}$ → $\frac{1}{4}$
0.652 × 1000 = 652	$\frac{652}{1000}$	$\frac{652}{1000}$ → $\frac{÷4}{÷4}$ → $\frac{163}{250}$

Real-Life Example

Kadim is the warehouse manager for CM Sports. He has a target to send out 80% of orders within 24 hours of them being received. On Monday, Kadim and his staff sent out 440 out of the 500 orders received. Have they reached their target?

1 Write 440 of 500 as a fraction:

$$\frac{440}{500}$$

2 Divide the numerator (top number) by the denominator (bottom number):

$$440 \div 500 = 0.88$$

3 Multiply the answer by 100:

$$0.88 \times 100 = 88$$

Kadim and his team hit their target. They sent out 88% of orders within the target time frame.

Practice

1 Express $\frac{1}{4}$ as a decimal.

2 Express 0.78 as a percentage.

3 Express $\frac{2}{5}$ as a percentage.

4 Express 0.52 as a fraction in its simplest form.

5 Express 63% as a decimal.

6 Express 80% as a fraction in its simplest form.

7 Asha is writing her university dissertation. She has to write a minimum of 15,000 words. She has currently written 9,864. What is this as a percentage of the minimum number of words?

Comparing Fractions, Decimals and Percentages

When comparing fractions, decimals and percentages, you need to convert all values to the same form, i.e. converting all values into decimals.

Put these values in order from smallest to largest.   75%   0.076 $\frac{5}{8}$

Make all values of the same form. In this example, it is easiest to convert all values to decimals.

Identify the order of decimals from smallest to largest.

Convert the values back to their original form.

75 % ⟶ $75 \div 100 = 0.75$

0.076 ⟶ 0.076

$\frac{5}{8}$ ⟶ $5 \div 8 = 0.625$

0.076   0.625   0.75

Smallest ⟶ Largest

0.076 $\frac{5}{8}$ 75%

Smallest ⟶ Largest

daydream
EDUCATION

Sometimes you may need to calculate fractions, decimals or percentages of amounts before making comparisons.

George is looking for a new lawnmower online. He has seen the lawnmower he wants on two websites, both of which have promotions. On which website is the lawnmower cheapest?

Website A

Lawnmower
£240
Promo:
Save $\frac{1}{3}$

Website B

Lawnmower
£199
Promo:
20% discount

1	Calculate the price of the lawnmower on website A:	$1 \div 3 \times 240 = 80$ $240 - 80 = £160$

2	Calculate the price of the lawnmower on website B:	$199 \times 0.2 = 39.80$ $199 - 39.80 = £159.20$

The lawnmower is 80p cheaper on website B.

Practice

1 Order the following fractions, decimals and percentages from smallest to largest.

46% $\frac{2}{3}$ 0.04 $\frac{8}{10}$ 86%   0.5

_____

_____

2 Three different shops are selling the same dress. Which one is cheapest?

Shop A:	Shop B:	Shop C:
£60 30% off	£50 $\frac{1}{4}$ off	£80 Half price

_____

_____

_____

_____

Ratios

A ratio is a way of comparing two or more quantities.

Purple paint is made by mixing blue and red paint in the ratio of 2 to 3.

2:3

To make mortar, sand and cement are mixed together in the ratio of 5 to 2.

5:2

Lilly, Jack and Jo have shared the money in the ratio of 2 to 6 to 3.

2:6:3

A ratio must be written in the correct order, with **the quantity mentioned first written first.**

The ratio of cats to dogs is 3:4. ✔

NOT

The ratio of dogs to cats is 3:4. ✘

Note that the ratio of dogs to cats is **4:3**.

Ratios are easier to work out when they are in their simplest form.
To simplify ratios, both numbers must be **divided by their highest common factor.**

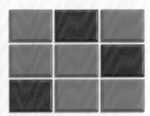

The ratio of blue to red tiles is 6 to 3 but this can be simplified.

3 is the highest common factor of 6 and 3, so divide both numbers by 3.

6:3
÷3   ÷3
2:1

Can you simplify these ratios to their simplest form?

6:4   **9:3**   **2:8:4**

daydream
EDUCATION

Dividing in a Ratio

Sometimes an amount needs to be divided according to a particular ratio.

Ava, **Isla** and **Freya** made **£315** selling burgers and hotdogs on a market stall. They agreed to split the money in the ratio of **3:2:4**. How much money does each person get?

1 Add the numbers in the ratio to calculate the total number of parts.

$$3 + 2 + 4 = 9$$

2 Find the value of 1 part by dividing the total amount by the total number of parts, 9.

$$315 \div 9 = 35$$
1 part = **35**

3 Multiply the value of 1 part, **35**, by the numbers in the ratio to calculate how much money each person gets.

$3 \times 35 = 105$
$2 \times 35 = 70$
$4 \times 35 = 140$

4 **315** divided in the ratio of **3:2:4** is **105:70:140** (note that ratios do not have units). Check your answer by adding together the values.

Ava	Isla	Freya
£105	£70	£140

$$105 + 70 + 140 = 315$$

If you know the value of one part of a ratio, you can calculate the values of the other parts, and the total sum of the ratio.

Nadia is a decorator. She needs to create a turquoise paint colour for her customer's new bathroom. To make turquoise paint, blue paint and green paint are mixed in the ratio of 4:7. If Nadia has 2.4 litres of blue paint, how much green paint does she need and how much turquoise paint can she make?

1 Calculate the value of 1 part by dividing the amount of blue paint by the number of blue parts in the ratio.

$$2.4 \div 4 = 0.6$$
1 part = 0.6

2 To calculate the amount of green paint that is needed, multiply the value of 1 part by the number of green parts in the ratio.

$$0.6 \times 7 = 4.2$$
Nadia needs 4.2 litres of green paint.

3 To calculate the amount of turquoise paint that Nadia can make, multiply the value of 1 part by the total number of parts in the ratio.

$$0.6 \times 11 = 6.6$$
Nadia can make 6.6 litres of turquoise paint.

Practice

Jack works in event management and is organising a festival. He has a budget of £5,000. He discovers a band called The Rockers, who agree to perform for a fee of £2,748.

1 (a) Bella, Harry and Rosie are all members of The Rockers. They agree to split the money in the ratio of 3:2:1. How much money will each band member receive?

_____

_____

_____

1 (b) Jack finds an AV business that will set up the staging and lighting for £1,388. The company sends a team of 2 live sound technicians and 3 lighting technicians. If the money is split in the ratio of 2:3, how much will each team receive?

_____

_____

Jack now has £864 left to pay four stewards: Dave, Ellie, Dan and Jade, who all worked different shifts at the festival. A breakdown of the stewards' shifts can be seen below.

Steward	Time Worked
Dave	8 hours
Ellie	8 hours
Dan	12 hours
Jade	20 hours

1 (c) How much will each steward be paid if they're all on the same hourly rate?

_____

_____

2 Katie is building a wall. She mixes sand and cement together in the ratio of 5:2 to make the mortar. If Katie has 15 kg of cement, how much sand will she need?

_____

_____

3 To make orange squash, Elliot mixes concentrated squash and water in the ratio of 1:5. If he has 2 litres of water, how much squash can Elliot make?

_____

_____

daydream EDUCATION

Proportion

Two quantities are in direct proportion if they increase or decrease at the same ratio, or at the same rate.

In the example below, the value of one variable is directly proportional to the other variable so, once the cost of one drink is known, you can calculate the cost of any number of drinks.

1 drink	3 drinks	152 drinks
×1.20	×1.20	×1.20
1 drink = 1.20	**3 drinks = 3.60**	**152 drinks = 182.40**
÷1.20	÷1.20	÷1.20

Real-Life Example 1

Mason is baking biscuits for a party. He knows that to make 30 biscuits he needs: 300 g of flour, 250 g of butter, 140 g of sugar and 2 eggs.

How much flour will Mason need for 45 biscuits?

1 Calculate how much flour is needed to make 1 biscuit.

$$\text{Flour in 1 biscuit} = \frac{\text{total amount of flour}}{\text{number of biscuits}} = \frac{300}{30} = 10$$

2 Calculate how much flour is needed for 45 biscuits.

$$10 \times 45 = 450$$

Mason will need 450 g of flour to make 45 biscuits.

Real-Life Example 2

Luke works for a British stationery company that has started to expand overseas. In January, the company sold $5,890.32 worth of pencils in the United States, which converted to £4,177.53.

Exchange rates express the value of one currency in terms of another.
For example, if £1 = $1.50, every £1 is worth $1.50.

a What was the exchange rate in January?

Calculate the exchange rate by dividing the US value by the UK equivalent.

$$\text{Exchange rate} = \frac{\text{US revenue}}{\text{UK equivalent}} = \frac{5,890.32}{4,177.53} = 1.41 \text{ (2 d.p.)}$$

b In the same month, the stationery company sold $6,732.79 worth of pens in the US. How much revenue did this generate in GBP?

Use the exchange rate to convert the US value into GBP.

$$6,732.79 \div 1.41 = 4,775.03$$

The company sold £4,775.02 worth of pens in the US in January.

43

Practice

1 Shelbi is a nail technician. She knows that 3 packs of 100 acrylic nail extensions cost £14.85. How much would 10 packs cost?

_____

_____

_____

_____

2 Sean is cooking spaghetti Bolognese. He has a list of basic ingredients that will serve 4 people, as shown below.

Ingredients	Quantity
Spaghetti	350 g
Chopped tomatoes	400 g
Mushrooms	90 g
Minced beef	500 g

What quantities of ingredients will Sean need to cook spaghetti Bolognese for himself and two friends?

_____

_____

_____

_____

3 Gemma pays £26.85 for three textbooks. How much will it cost her to buy two more books at the same price?

_____

_____

_____

_____

_____

daydream
EDUCATION

Solving Equations

An **equation** states that two things are **equal** and will, therefore, always contain an equals sign, =.

Equations are used to find unknown values, or variables. In an equation, variables are represented using letters or symbols. Look at the examples below.

| $n + 3 = 12$ | $x - 7 = 1$ | $5y = 20$ | $\dfrac{m}{5} = 3$ |

Solving an equation involves finding the value of the variable.
This is done by "undoing" the equation using inverse, or opposite, operations.

Addition and Subtraction are inverse operations.

$+4$ **12** -4

$8 + 4 = 12$
$12 - 4 = 8$

8

Multiplication and Division are inverse operations.

$\times 5$ **15** $\div 5$

$3 \times 5 = 15$
$15 \div 5 = 3$

3

The aim when solving an equation is to get the variable by itself on one side of the equation with a number on the other side – for example, $x = 2$.

This is done by performing the opposite of the operation acting upon the variable **to both sides of the equation**. Look at the examples below.

$n + 3 = 12$	$x - 7 = 1$	$5 \times y = 20$	$m \div 5 = 3$
$-3 \qquad -3$	$+7 \qquad +7$	$\div 5 \qquad \div 5$	$\times 5 \qquad \times 5$
$n = 9$	$x = 8$	$y = 4$	$m = 15$

The above rules do not always work for division and subtraction.
When the variable is the divisor, or being subtracted, solve the problem in two steps.

When the variable is being subtracted:

Add d to both sides of the equation.

$$7 - d = 4$$
$$+d \qquad +d$$
$$7 \quad = 4 + d$$

Subtract 4 from both sides of the equation.

$$-4 \qquad -4$$
$$3 \quad = d$$

When the variable is the divisor:

Multiply both sides of the equation by w.

$$\frac{12}{w} = 3$$
$$\times w \qquad \times w$$
$$12 \quad = 3w$$

Divide both sides of the equation by 3.

$$\div 3 \qquad \div 3$$
$$4 \quad = w$$

45

Using Equations to Solve Real-Life Problems

Equations can be used to help solve real-life problems.

Max and Amy work in a hair salon. Over the weekend, they have 37 appointments in total. If Amy has 21 appointments, how many does Max have?

1. Turn the question into an equation.

Use m to represent the unknown value (the number of appointments Max has).	Max has __ appts Amy has 21 appts 37 appts in total
	$m + 21 = 37$

2. Solve the equation to find the value of m.

Subtraction is the inverse operation of addition so **subtract 21 from both sides of the equation.**	$m + 21 = 37$ $-21 \quad -21$ $m = 16$

The equation is now solved. m = **16**, so Max has 16 appointments.

Rohan has three pieces of wood of equal length, and one 6 cm piece. The total length of the four pieces of wood is 42 cm.

How long is each of the three equal pieces of wood?

1. Turn the question into an equation.

Use w to represent the unknown value (the length of the three equal pieces of wood).	3 pieces of wood Other piece of wood Total length
	$3 \times w + 6 = 42$

2. Solve the equation to find the value of w.

Subtraction is the inverse operation of addition so **subtract 6 from both sides of the equation.**	$3w + 6 = 42$ $-6 \quad -6$ $3w = 36$
Division is the inverse operation of multiplication so **divide both sides of the equation by 3.**	$\div 3 \qquad \div 3$ $w = 12$

The equation is now solved. w = **12**, so each equal piece of wood is 12 cm long.

daydream EDUCATION

Solve the following equations.

1 (a) $\quad x + 11 = 21$	1 (b) $\quad 3y - 5 = 16$
1 (c) $\quad \dfrac{m}{5} + 4 = 9$	1 (d) $\quad \dfrac{24}{w} = 4$

2 Marie's catering company has been asked to make sandwiches for an upcoming conference. She needs to make three sandwiches per delegate, plus an additional 25 for the staff. Marie has made 403 sandwiches. How many delegates are attending the conference?

3 James is a plasterer. He had six packs of plasterboards but one of his colleagues has used three individual boards. He now has 27 plasterboards in total. How many plasterboards were there in a pack?

4 Mason is the organiser of a music festival. He arranges for seven teams of 12 stewards to work at the festival. On the day, only 79 stewards turn up. How many stewards were missing?

Formulae

A formula is an equation that shows the relationship between different variables. Formulae can be written in words, letters or symbols.

The **speed of an object** can be calculated using the formula:

$$speed = \frac{distance}{time}$$

$$s = \frac{d}{t}$$

A person's **total pay** can be calculated using the formula:

$$total\ pay = hours \times wage$$

$$p = h \times w$$

The **area of a circle** can be calculated using the formula:

$$area\ of\ circle = \pi \times radius^2$$

$$A = \pi r^2$$

Solving Problems Using Formulae

Sometimes, solving a problem involves substituting numbers into a formula.

Will gets paid £15 an hour. If he works for 6 hours, how much does he get paid?	**Total Pay = Hours × Wage**

1 Substitute the known numbers into the formula.

Total Pay = 6 × £15

2 Follow the rules of **BIDMAS** to find the answer.

Total Pay = £90

Convert 86°F from Fahrenheit to Celsius.

$$C = \frac{5(f - 32)}{9}$$

1 Substitute the known numbers into the formula.

$$C = \frac{5(86 - 32)}{9}$$

2 Follow the rules of **BIDMAS** to find the answer.

$$C = \frac{5(54)}{9} \blacktriangleright C = \frac{270}{9} \blacktriangleright C = 30°C$$

The cooking time for a chicken is 30 minutes per kilogram (kg), plus 40 minutes. What is the cooking time for a chicken that weighs 1.5 kg?

Cooking Time = 30 × weight + 40

T = 30w + 40

1 Substitute the known numbers into the formula.

T = (30 × 1.5) + 40

2 Follow the rules of **BIDMAS** to find the answer.

T = 45 + 40
T = 85 mins

---

daydream EDUCATION

Rearranging Formulae

Sometimes you will need to rearrange a formula before solving a problem. Look at how the formula for speed can be rearranged to make either distance or time the subject:

speed = $\dfrac{\text{distance}}{\text{time}}$	distance = speed × time	time = $\dfrac{\text{distance}}{\text{speed}}$

Real-Life Examples

George drove for 3 hours at a speed of 32 miles per hour.
How far did he travel?

Jo ran 100 metres at a speed of 8 metres per second.
What was her time?

1 Rearrange the formula so **distance** is the subject.

$$s = \frac{d}{t}$$

$$\times t \qquad \times t$$

$$s \times t = d$$

1 Rearrange the formula so **time** is the subject.

$$s = \frac{d}{t}$$

$$\times t \qquad \times t$$

$$s \times t = d$$

$$\div s \qquad \div s$$

$$t = \frac{d}{s}$$

2 Substitute the known values into the formula and solve.

$$32 \times 3 = d$$

$$96 = d$$

George drove 96 miles.

2 Substitute the known values into the formula and solve.

$$t = \frac{100}{8}$$

$$t = 12.5$$

Jo's time was 12.5 seconds.

Practice

1 It took Beth 5 hours to travel 320 km from London to Chester. Calculate her average speed.

2 Freddie is switching TV provider. The monthly subscription fee is £14.99, and he has to pay a one-off £49 setup fee. Calculate the total cost over 1 year.

3 Gwen is going on holiday to Florida. Her weather app tells her that it is currently 32°C. Rearrange the formula below and calculate the temperature in Fahrenheit.

Degrees Celsius = $\dfrac{5(\text{Fahrenheit} - 32)}{9}$

2D & 3D Shapes

2D or two-dimensional shapes are flat. They have two dimensions: length and width.

Triangles
3 sides

Right Angle	Isosceles	Equilateral	Scalene
One angle = 90°	2 equal sides and 2 equal angles	3 equal sides and 3 equal angles	No equal sides and no equal angles

Quadrilaterals
4 sides

Rectangle	Kite	Parallelogram	Trapezium

Other Shapes

Circle	Pentagon	Hexagon	Octagon

3D or three-dimensional shapes have three dimensions: length, width and height.

Cube
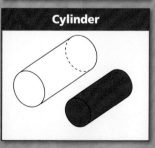

Cuboid
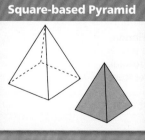

Triangular Prism
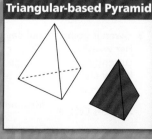

Cylinder
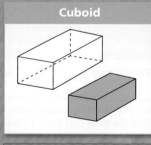

Square-based Pyramid

Triangular-based Pyramid
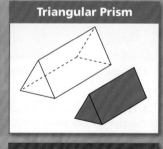

daydream EDUCATION

Symmetry

Line Symmetry

A line of symmetry, also known as a line of reflection, divides an object into two parts that are the same size and shape.

A square has 4 lines of symmetry.	An equilateral triangle has 3 lines of symmetry.	A regular pentagon has 5 lines of symmetry.

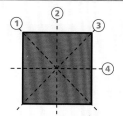
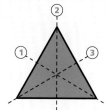
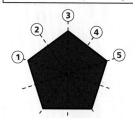

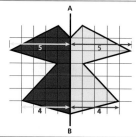

This shape has one line of symmetry. All corresponding parts are equidistant from the line of symmetry.

The butterfly offers an example of line symmetry that occurs in nature. It has one line of symmetry.

Practice

1

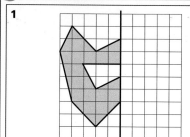

Can you complete this shape? Remember, all corresponding parts should be equidistant from the line of symmetry.

2

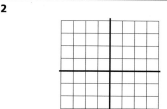

Justin is tiling his bathroom using four different coloured tiles. Create a pattern above using all of the tiles that are symmetrical through both lines of symmetry.

Solids and Their Nets

A solid figure has flat surfaces (faces), edges and corners (vertices). A net is the surface of a solid 3D shape folded out flat. It is a 2D representation of a 3D figure.

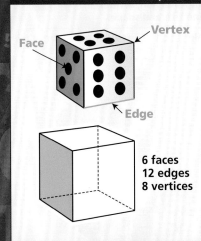

Face
Vertex
Edge

6 faces
12 edges
8 vertices

Net of cube
The net of an object can often be configured in several ways.

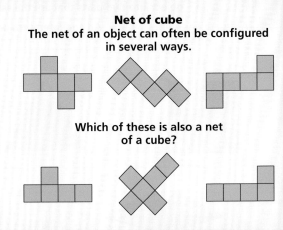

Which of these is also a net of a cube?

Cuboid

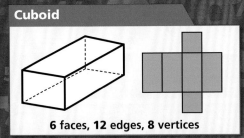

6 faces, 12 edges, 8 vertices

Triangular Prism

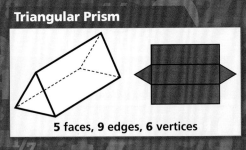

5 faces, 9 edges, 6 vertices

Square-based Pyramid

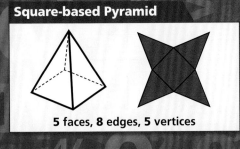

5 faces, 8 edges, 5 vertices

Triangular-based Pyramid

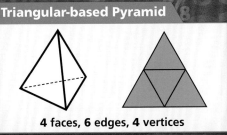

4 faces, 6 edges, 4 vertices

The surface area of a solid figure is equal to the total area of its net. To work out the surface area of a shape add together the areas of the separate faces of the net.

daydream EDUCATION

Daniel works for a packaging company. His customer has asked for a rectangular box with the following dimensions:

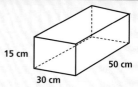

15 cm
50 cm
30 cm

Width: 30 cm   Height: 15 cm   Length: 50 cm

Help Daniel work out the net of the box so that he can create a template for production.

To solve this problem, follow the steps outlined below.

1 A cuboid has 6 rectangular faces. Draw the top face first, with the dimensions 30 cm × 50 cm.

50 cm
30 cm

2 Draw the side rectangular faces on either side of the top face. The dimensions of these faces are 15 cm × 50 cm.

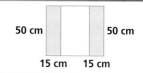

50 cm   50 cm
15 cm   15 cm

3 Add the bottom face to the side of one of the side faces. The dimension of this face is 30 cm × 50 cm (the same as the top face). In this example, the face has been added to the left side but it could also have been added to the right side.

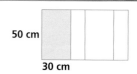

50 cm
30 cm

4 Finally, add the front and back faces. These can be placed in various places. However, in this example, they have been added to the first face. The dimensions of these faces are 30 cm × 15 cm.

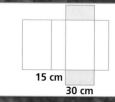

15 cm
30 cm

Practice

1 Daniel's customer also requires a much smaller triangular postal tube. The required dimensions are shown below. Draw a net of the box in the grid provided.

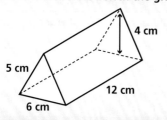

4 cm
5 cm
12 cm
6 cm

2 cm

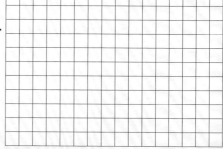

Elevations of 3D Shapes

Elevations are 2D representations of 3D shapes.

Plans and Elevations of 3D Shapes

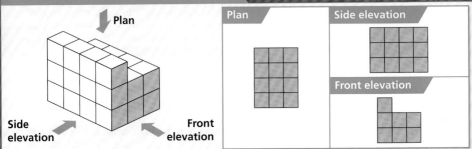

Real-Life Example

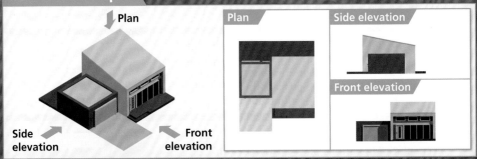

Practice

1 Which of the following is the correct side elevation of the shape below?

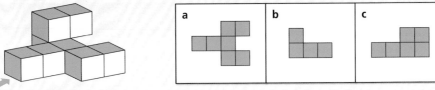

2 Draw the plan, side elevation and front elevation of the shape below.

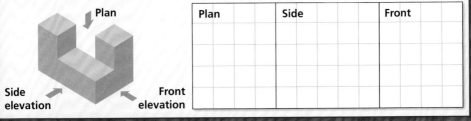

Plan	Side	Front

daydream
EDUCATION

Plans

Plan drawings are often used to show the layout of an area, such as a building or garden. The plan is drawn at a scale, proportional to the real-life size. If the ratio of A to B is 1:2, A is half the size of B.

Oliver is a carpet-fitter. He has the following plan of a client's bedroom, drawn at a scale of 1:50. This means that the bedroom is 50 times bigger in real life than in the drawing. To accurately fit the carpet, Oliver needs to know the real-life measurement of x.

0   50 cm
Scale 1:50

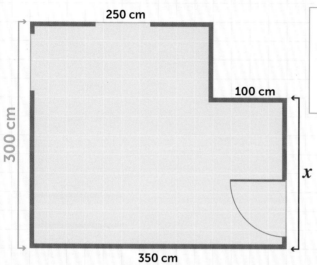

250 cm

100 cm

300 cm

x

350 cm

To identify the length of **300 cm** on the drawing, measure the length using a ruler or divide the real-life measurement by the scale:

300 cm $\div 50 =$ **6 cm**

To identify the length of x in real life, use a ruler to measure the length of x on the drawing (in this case 4 cm) and multiply it by the scale:

4 cm $\times 50 =$ **200 cm**

A plan drawing of a flat is shown below.

1 m
Scale 1:200

Master Bedroom

Bath 2

Bath 1

Kitchen

Bedroom 2

Bedroom 3

Lounge

The **kitchen** measures 2.75 cm × 2.5 cm on the diagram, which is 550 cm × 500 cm in real life.

The **lounge** measures 2.5 cm × 2.5 cm on the diagram, which is 500 cm × 500 cm in real life.

To identify the real-life dimensions of the **master bedroom**, multiply the actual measurements by the scale:

2.75 cm × 200 = 550
2.5 cm × 200 = 500
so the real life dimensions of the master bedroom are
550 cm × 550 cm or 5.5 m × 5 m

Practice

1 Marcus is planning to build a swimming pool. His scale drawing of the pool measures 10 cm by 20 cm. The scale factor is 1:50. What are the dimensions of the actual swimming pool?

_____

_____

2 Anna is landscaping her garden. Her plan is shown below.

0.5 m

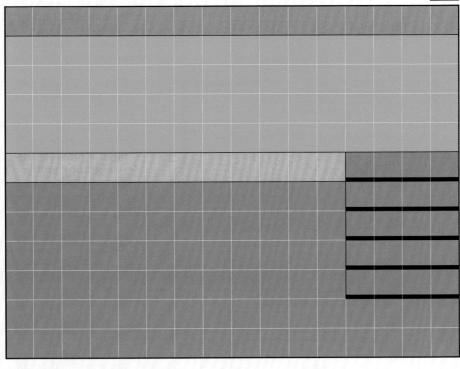

2 (a) What area of Anna's garden is grass (green area on plan)?

_____

_____

2 (b) Anna wants to put a shed and a table on her patio (grey area on plan). Does she have enough room? She will not be able to place either item over the steps to the right of the patio.   Table: 1 m × 2 m   Shed: 3 m × 2 m

_____

_____

_____

daydream
EDUCATION

Maps

Maps show an area reduced in size. This is measured using a scale, which is the ratio of a model dimension to the real-life dimension.

Using Scales to Draw and Read Maps

The map below has a scale of **1:50,000**.
This means the map is 50,000 times smaller than the actual area shown.

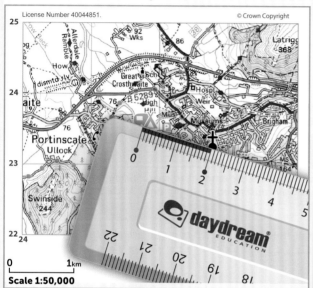

License Number 40044851.
© Crown Copyright

Scale 1:50,000

On the map the campsite is 2 cm from the church. To calculate the actual distance, multiply the measurement by the scale:

2 cm × **Scale**
2 cm × **50,000 = 100,000 cm**

Convert the measurement to the correct unit:

100,000 cm = **1 km**

Therefore, the campsite is 1 km from the church.

Practice

Scale 1:1,000,000

1 This map has a scale of 1:1,000,000. On the map, measure the distance from Manchester to Liverpool and calculate the actual distance in kilometres.

Perimeter & Area

Perimeter is the total distance around a shape's outer edge.
To calculate the perimeter of a shape, add together the lengths of all the sides.

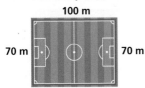

100 m
70 m | 70 m
100 m

The perimeter of the football field is 340 m:
100 + 100 + 70 + 70 = **340 m**

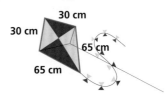

30 cm
30 cm
65 cm
65 cm

The perimeter of the kite is 190 cm:
30 + 30 + 65 + 65 = **190 cm**

Area

Area is the total size of a flat surface. It is the amount of space inside the perimeter.
Area is 2-dimensional, so it is always measured in square units, such as cm² or m².

Rectangle/Square

What is the area of the football field?

70 m
100 m

Area of rectangle = *length* × *width*
= 100 × 70
Area of field = **7,000 m²**

Triangle

What is the area of the sign?

24 cm
32 cm

Area of triangle = $\frac{1}{2}$ × *base* × *height*
= $\frac{1}{2}$ × 32 × 24
Area of sign = **384 cm²**

Parallelogram

What is the area of the side face of the rubber?

7 mm
38 mm

Area of parallelogram = *base* × *height*
= 38 × 7
Area of side face = **266 mm²**

Trapezium

What is the area of the roof?

10 m   *a*
5 m
15 m   *b*

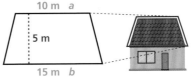

Area of trapezium = $\frac{1}{2}$ × (*a* + *b*) × *height*
= $\frac{1}{2}$ × (10 + 15) × 5
= $\frac{1}{2}$ × (25) × 5
Area of roof = **62.5 m²**

daydream
EDUCATION

Calculating the Circumference & Area of a Circle

The perimeter of a circle is called the circumference. To calculate the circumference, you need to use π (pi). π is an irrational number that never ends or repeats: 3.14159265359...

You may be given the number of decimal places to use for π in the question. If not, use 3.14. If your calculator has a π button, you can also use that. Using π or 3.14 will give you slightly different answers, but both will be marked as correct.

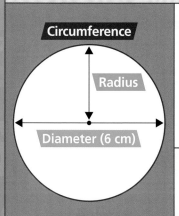

Circumference

Radius

Diameter (6 cm)

Circumference = π × Diameter ($C = \pi d$)

$\qquad$ = 3.14 × 6

$\qquad$ = 18.84 cm

OR

Circumference = 2 × π × Radius ($C = 2\pi r$)

$\qquad$ = 2 × 3.14 × 3

$\qquad$ = 18.84 cm

The radius is half the diameter.

The area of a circle can be calculated using the radius:

Area = π × Radius × Radius ($A = \pi r^2$)

$\qquad$ = 3.14 × 3 × 3

$\qquad$ = 28.26 cm²

Practice

1 (a) Oscar is planning to put up a fence all the way around the edge of his garden. How many metres of fencing will he need?

10 m

4 m

1 (b) Oscar is now considering gravelling the whole of his garden. What is the area of Oscar's garden?

2 Saskia is going for a run around her local park. She wants to run for 10 km. How many laps of the park will Saskia have to run to reach her goal? Use 3.14 for π in all calculations.

Park

400 m

3 Katherine is selling her handmade jewellery at a local market. A customer asks if the area of the pendant on a necklace is smaller than 1 cm². What should Katherine reply? Use 3.14 for π in all calculations.

0.5 cm

Area of Compound Shapes

When measuring the area of a compound shape, break it down into simpler shapes and then add the areas together.

Example 1

Look at the plan of the room below. Calculate the area.

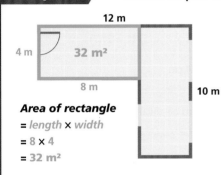

12 m

4 m

32 m²

8 m

10 m

Area of rectangle
= *length* × *width*
= 8 × 4
= 32 m²

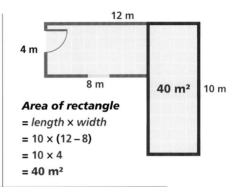

12 m

4 m

8 m

40 m² 10 m

Area of rectangle
= *length* × *width*
= 10 × (12 – 8)
= 10 × 4
= 40 m²

Total area of the compound shape: 32 + 40 = 72 m²

To calculate the perimeter, add together the sides. The sides not labelled can be calculated by using the sides that are labelled.

8 + 4 + 12 + 10 + (12 – 8) + (10 – 4)
8 + 4 + 12 + 10 + 4 + 6 = 44 m

Example 2

Sophia is laying a new lawn in her back garden.
A plan of the garden is shown below. Calculate the area of the garden.

Area of rectangle = *length* × *width*
= 12 × 3
= **36 m²**

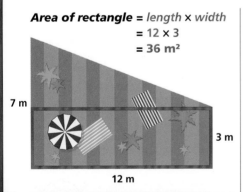

7 m

3 m

12 m

Area of triangle = $\frac{1}{2}$ × *base* × *height*
= $\frac{1}{2}$ × 12 × (7 - 3)
= $\frac{1}{2}$ × 12 × 4
= **24 m²**

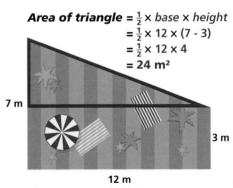

7 m

3 m

12 m

Total area of garden = 36 + 24 = 60 m²

daydream EDUCATION

1 Shannon is painting the side of a building. She has two 10 litre tins of paint. If 1 litre of paint covers 6 m², will Shannon have enough paint to paint the side of the building?

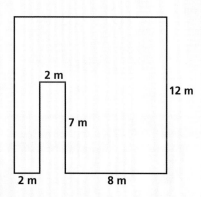

_____

_____

_____

_____

_____

_____

2 (a) Ryan is fitting laminate wood flooring for a customer. The laminate costs £15 per m². Calculate the total cost of the laminate flooring.

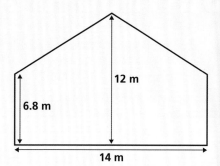

_____

_____

_____

_____

_____

_____

2 (b) Ryan also needs to fit a skirting board along the edge of the floor. He buys skirting in packs of 2400 mm. How many packs will Ryan need to buy?

_____

_____

_____

3 Kurt needs to re-turf his lawn. He has a budget of £300, and the turf he wants costs £3 per m². Does Kurt have enough money to buy the turf he wants?

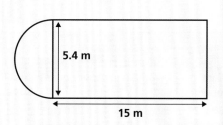

_____

_____

_____

_____

_____

_____

Surface Area

Surface area is the total area of the outer surface of a 3D object. The surface area of a solid figure is equal to the total area of its net.

To calculate the surface area of a shape, work out the area of each face and add them together. In some questions, the areas of a shape's faces may already be given to you.

Triangular Prism

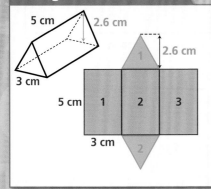

1 Calculate the areas of the different sized faces:

Area = $l \times w$	Area = $\frac{1}{2} \times b \times h$
= 5 × 3	= $\frac{1}{2}$ × 3 × 2.6
= 15 cm²	= 3.9 cm²

2 Multiply these areas by the number of corresponding faces:

15 × 3 = 45 cm²   3.9 × 2 = 7.8 cm²

3 Add the areas together: 45 + 7.8 = 52.8 cm²

Square-based Pyramid

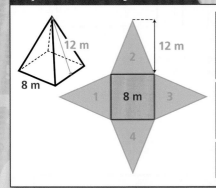

1 Calculate the areas of the different sized faces:

Area = $l \times w$	Area = $\frac{1}{2} \times b \times h$
= 8 × 8	= $\frac{1}{2}$ × 8 × 12
= 64 m²	= 48 m²

2 Multiply the area of the triangular face by the number of corresponding faces:

48 × 4 = 192 m²

3 Add the areas together: 192 + 64 = 256 m².

Real-Life Example 1

Sam makes wooden jewellery boxes. Calculate the area of wood needed by Sam to make the box shown.

30 × 20 = 600   600 × 2 = 1,200 cm²
8 × 20 = 160   160 × 2 = 320 cm²
8 × 30 = 240   240 × 2 = 480 cm²

1200 + 320 + 480 = 2,000 cm²

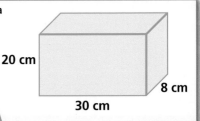

Sam would need 2,000 cm² of wood to make the box.

daydream EDUCATION

An upholstery company is making cushion covers for their new range of bolster sofa cushions. Work out how much fabric the company will need to cover 500 cushions.

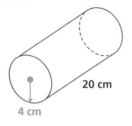

20 cm

4 cm

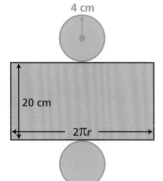

4 cm

20 cm

2πr

1 Calculate the areas of the different faces. The cylindrical cushion has three faces: 2 circles and a rectangle.

Area = 2πrh	**Area = πr²**
= 2 × 3.14 × 4 × 20	= 3.14 × 4²
= **502.4 cm²**	= 50.24 cm²

The length of the rectangle is equal to the circumference of the end circle.

2 Multiply the area of the circular face by the number of corresponding faces:

50.24 cm² × **2** = 100.48 cm²

3 Add the areas of the faces:

502.4 + 100.48 = **602.88 cm²**

4 Multiply the surface area of one cushion by the total number of cushions that need to be covered:

602.88 × 500 = 301,440 cm²

The company will need 301,440 cm² of fabric to cover 500 cushions.

Practice

1 (a) A confectionary company sells tubes of sweets. They want to change the shape of their packaging to attract the attention of shoppers. Which packaging would require more material to make? Use 3.14 for π in all calculations.

2 cm

14 cm

6.5 cm

4 cm

Existing packaging

New packaging

_____

_____

_____

_____

_____

_____

1 (b) The confectionary company is also considering packaging sweets in a cubic cardboard box. If each side of the box measures 5 cm, how much cardboard would be needed?

_____

_____

Volume

Volume is the amount of space inside a 3D shape or object.

Prisms and Cylinders

Solid objects that maintain a constant cross-sectional area along their length.

Volume of prism or cylinder = cross-sectional area × length

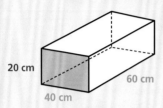

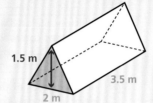

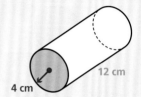

20 cm 40 cm 60 cm

1.5 m 2 m 3.5 m

4 cm 12 cm

$V = w \times h \times l$
$= 40 \times 20 \times 60$
$= 48,000 \text{ cm}^3$

$V = \frac{1}{2} \times b \times h \times l$
$= \frac{1}{2} \times 2 \times 1.5 \times 3.5$
$= 5.25 \text{ m}^3$

$V = \pi r^2 \times l$
$= \pi \times 16 \times 12$
$= 603.19 \text{ cm}^3 \text{ (2 d.p.)}$

Real-Life Example

Zoe works in a pet shop that has just invested in a new fishtank. What is the volume of the fishtank?

Volume = $w \times h \times l$
Volume = $50 \times 25 \times 30 = 37,500 \text{ cm}^3$

So, the volume of the fishtank is 37,500 cm³.

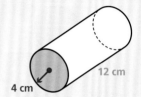

25 cm 50 cm 30 cm

Zoe uses a jug to fill the tank with water. How many jugs of water will it take to fill the whole tank?

Volume = $\pi r^2 \times l$
Volume = $\pi \times 6^2 \times 13 = 1,470.27 \text{ cm}^3 \text{ (2 d.p.)}$

Divide the volume of the tank by the volume of the jug to identify how many jugs of water are needed to fill the fishtank: $37,500 \div 1,470.27 = 25.51 \text{ (2 d.p)}$

It will take 25.51 jugs of water to fill the fishtank.

6 cm 13 cm

daydream EDUCATION

Practice

1 Chloe works in a post office. She needs to know the volume of 3 different parcels so that she can assign the correct postage labels to each. The table below shows the post office's maximum volume for each parcel size.

Small parcel	Medium parcel	Large parcel
25,200 cm³	129,076 cm³	1,000,000 cm³

The parcels Chloe needs to label are:

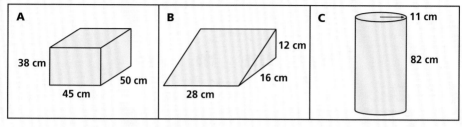

A 38 cm, 45 cm, 50 cm

B 12 cm, 16 cm, 28 cm

C 11 cm, 82 cm

What label should each parcel have?

_____

_____

_____

_____

_____

_____

2 Mark is fitting a new bathroom and needs to hire a skip to throw away any waste. The hire company offers two different-sized skips for domestic use. Mark estimates that he will need a skip with a capacity of at least 4 m³. Which skip will best meet Mark's requirements?

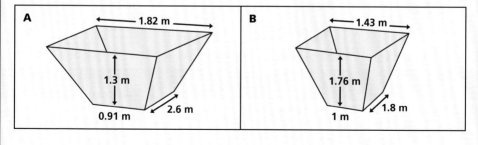

A 1.82 m, 1.3 m, 0.91 m, 2.6 m

B 1.43 m, 1.76 m, 1 m, 1.8 m

_____

_____

_____

_____

Measures

Length

The metric units of length are:
millimetres (mm), **centimetres (cm)**, **metres (m)** and **kilometres (km)**.

10 mm = 1 cm   **100 cm = 1 m**   **1,000 m = 1 km**

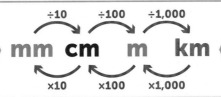

Although division is used to convert to a larger unit, this does not mean that 1 mm is longer than 1 cm.
1 mm is ten times shorter than 1 cm.

÷10   ÷100   ÷1,000

mm   cm   m   km

×10   ×100   ×1,000

Although multiplication is used to convert to a smaller unit, this does not mean that 1 km is shorter than 1 m.
1 km is 1,000 times longer than 1 m.

Real-Life Examples

Ellis is competing in the long jump at an athletics competition. He jumps **2.25 m**. How far did Ellis jump in **cm**?

To convert **2.25 m** to **cm**, multiply by 100.

2.25 × 100 = 225 cm

In the same competition, Jessica ran in the **12,000 m** race. How far did Jessica run in **km**?

To convert **12,000 m** to **km**, divide by 1,000.

12,000 ÷ 1,000 = 12 km

Weight

The metric units of weight are:
grams (g) and **kilograms (kg)**.

1,000 g = 1 kg

÷1,000

g   kg

×1,000

750 g = 0.75 kg   **5,000 g = 5 kg**   **80,000 g = 80 kg**

Real-Life Examples

Liz is going on holiday. The luggage weight limit on her flight is **20 kg**. Her case weighs **23,000 g**. Is Liz's case over the limit?

To convert **20 kg** to **g**, multiply by 1,000.

20 × 1,000 = 20,000 g

Liz's case is **3000 g** over the weight limit.

Neil needs **1 kg** of flour to bake a cake. He has **100 g**. Is this enough?

To convert **100 g** to **kg**, divide by 1,000.

100 ÷ 1,000 = 0.1 kg

Neil does not have enough flour.

daydream EDUCATION

The metric units of capacity are:
millilitres (ml) and **litres (l)**.

$$1,000 \text{ ml} = 1 \text{ l}$$

÷1,000

ml **l**

×1,000

100 ml = 0.1 l   330 ml = 0.33 l   20,000 ml = 20 l

Real-Life Examples

Tim buys **13 l** of lemonade for a party. The guests drink **9,500 ml** of lemonade. How many litres of lemonade does Tim have left?

To convert **9,500 ml** to l, divide by 1,000.

9,500 ÷ 1,000 = 9.5 l
13 − 9.5 = 3.5

Tim has **3.5 l** of lemonade left.

Dylan is filling up his **50,000 ml** fishtank with water. The jug he is using holds **4 l**. How many jugs will Dylan need to fill the tank?

To convert **4 l** to ml, multiply by 1,000.

4 × 1,000 = 4,000 ml

50,000 ÷ 4,000 = 12.5

Dylan will need **12.5** jugs to fill the tank.

Practice

1 (a) Harry is a lorry driver. He has to travel a distance of 56.8 km. He has so far driven 27,530 metres. How many kilometres does Harry have left to drive?

1 (b) Harry's lorry can carry a maximum weight of 13,500 kg. He is transporting pallets of clothing that weigh 181,442 g each. What is the maximum amount of pallets the lorry can carry?

2 Jenna's coffee shop sold 640 caramel lattes in the past month. Each caramel latte includes 35 ml of syrup. The syrup is sold in 2.5 litre bottles. To the nearest whole number, how many bottles of syrup have been used in the past month?

Metric to Imperial
Measurement Conversion

To convert between metric and imperial units of measure, multiply or divide by the conversion factors shown below.

Length

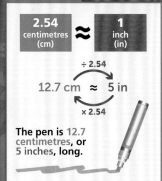

2.54 centimetres (cm) ≈ **1** inch (in)

÷ 2.54
12.7 cm ≈ 5 in
× 2.54

The pen is 12.7 centimetres, or 5 inches, long.

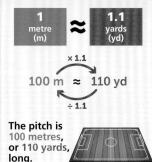

1 metre (m) ≈ **1.1** yards (yd)

× 1.1
100 m ≈ 110 yd
÷ 1.1

The pitch is 100 metres, or 110 yards, long.

1.6 kilometres (km) ≈ **1** mile (mi)

÷ 1.6
184 km ≈ 115 mi
× 1.6

It is 184 kilometres, or 115 miles, from Bath to London.

Real-Life Example

Daisy wants to run 11 miles for her marathon training. Her GPS watch only records in kilometres. How far does Daisy need to run in kilometres to reach her target of 11 miles?

To convert from miles to kilometres, multiply by 1.6.

$11 \times 1.6 = 17.6$.
So, Daisy needs to run 17.6 km.

Weight

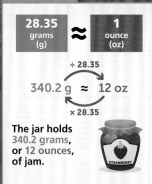

28.35 grams (g) ≈ **1** ounce (oz)

÷ 28.35
340.2 g ≈ 12 oz
× 28.35

The jar holds 340.2 grams, or 12 ounces, of jam.

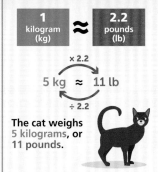

1 kilogram (kg) ≈ **2.2** pounds (lb)

× 2.2
5 kg ≈ 11 lb
÷ 2.2

The cat weighs 5 kilograms, or 11 pounds.

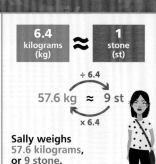

6.4 kilograms (kg) ≈ **1** stone (st)

÷ 6.4
57.6 kg ≈ 9 st
× 6.4

Sally weighs 57.6 kilograms, or 9 stone.

Real-Life Example

Sian is making pancakes. The recipe says she needs 200 grams of flour. Her weighing scales only measure in ounces. How many ounces of flour will Sian need?

To convert from grams to ounces, divide by 28.35.

$200 \div 28.35 = 7$ (1 s.f.)
Sian will need 7 oz of flour to make the pancakes.

daydream EDUCATION

Capacity

568 millilitres (ml)	≈	1 pint (pt)

$$÷ 568$$
$$1,136 \text{ ml} ≈ 2 \text{ pt}$$
$$× 568$$

1 litre (l)	≈	1.76 pints (pt)

$$× 1.76$$
$$2 l ≈ 3.52 \text{ pt}$$
$$÷ 1.76$$

4.5 litres (l)	≈	1 gallon (gal)

$$÷ 4.5$$
$$180 l ≈ 40 \text{ gal}$$
$$× 4.5$$

The jug has a capacity of **1,136 millilitres, or 2 pints.**

The carton has a capacity of **2 litres, or 3.52 pints.**

The bath has a capacity of **180 litres, or 40 gallons.**

Real-Life Example

Eric works in a supermarket. He finds a 4-pint bottle of milk that has passed its sell-by date. The stock write-off sheet asks for the amount in litres. How many litres have been written off?

To convert from pints to litres, divide by 1.76.

$4 ÷ 1.76 = 2.27$ **(2 d.p.)**
So, 2.27 litres of milk have been written off.

Practice

1 (a) The tank of Ruth's car holds 55 litres. She goes to a petrol station that charges £5.36 per gallon. How much will it cost Ruth to fill her car with a full tank of petrol?

1 (b) Ruth drives home from the petrol station on the motorway at a speed of 65 mph. What is Ruth's speed in km/h?

2 Terry is a weightlifter. At the start of his 12-week training programme, he weighs 93.44 kg. Terry aims to gain 0.75 lbs of muscle per week. How much will Terry weigh, in kilograms, by the end of his 12-week training programme if he achieves his goal?

3 Ben is a kitchen fitter. He is ordering worktops for a customer. He needs a total length of 205 inches. His supplier has the following lengths available:
100 cm @ £75   200 cm @ £105   300 cm @ £150
What is the most cost effective way for Ben to order the worktops?

Time

60 seconds = 1 minute	7 days = 1 week
60 minutes = 1 hour	52 weeks = 1 year
24 hours = 1 day	100 years = 1 century

Analogue Clocks

The short hand is the hour hand. It takes 1 hour to move from one number to the next.

The long hand is the minute hand. It takes 60 minutes to go all the way around the clock.

The 12 longer or bolder lines on a clock each represent 1 hour intervals for the hour hand, or 5 minute intervals for the minute hand.

The 60 small lines on a clock each represent one minute. It takes the minute hand 60 seconds to move between each pair of lines.

7:10
Ten minutes past seven.

3:20
Twenty minutes past three.

10:50
Ten minutes to eleven.

Practice

What time is displayed on the clocks below?

1 (a)

1 (b)

1 (c)

_____   _____   _____

Draw the following times on the clocks below.

2 (a)

6:15

2 (b)

11:50

2 (c)

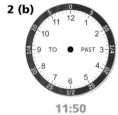

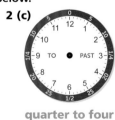

quarter to four

daydream EDUCATION

Digital clocks display the time digitally as numbers.

On a 12-hour digital clock, 12 hours are a.m. (morning) and 12 hours are p.m. (afternoon).

On a 24-hour digital clock, there are 24 hours and no a.m. or p.m.

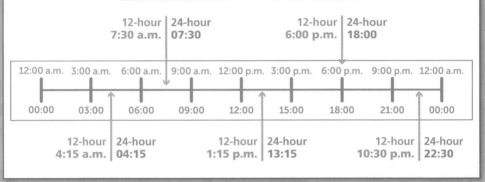

12-hour	24-hour
7:30 a.m.	07:30

12-hour	24-hour
6:00 p.m.	18:00

12:00 a.m.	3:00 a.m.	6:00 a.m.	9:00 a.m.	12:00 p.m.	3:00 p.m.	6:00 p.m.	9:00 p.m.	12:00 a.m.
00:00	03:00	06:00	09:00	12:00	15:00	18:00	21:00	00:00

12-hour	24-hour
4:15 a.m.	04:15

12-hour	24-hour
1:15 p.m.	13:15

12-hour	24-hour
10:30 p.m.	22:30

Real-Life Examples

Filip has a job interview at 14:30. How is this time displayed on a 12-hour clock?

To convert a 24-hour afternoon time to a 12-hour format, subtract 12 hours and add p.m.

14:30 − 12:00 = 2:30 p.m.

14:30 = 2:30 p.m.

Nicole needs to catch a bus at 8 p.m. It is now 19:05. Has she missed the bus?

To convert a 12-hour afternoon time to a 24-hour format, add 12 hours and remove p.m.

8:00 + 12:00 = 20:00

8 p.m. = 20:00, so Nicole has not missed the bus.

Practice

Complete the following conversions.

1 (a) 3:20 a.m. = _____   **1 (b)** _____ = 00:05   **1 (c)** _____ = 19:38

2 Gabriela is going to the cinema. The film she wants to watch starts at 17:00. It takes Gabriela 1 hour to get to the cinema. The time is 4:15 p.m. Will she get to the cinema before the film starts?

_____

Time Intervals

Ethan left his house at 6:45 a.m. His journey to work took him 1 hour and 32 minutes. What time did he arrive in work?

1 Identify what information is required to answer the question.

You are given the start time and the duration, so you need to find the end time.

2 Break down the duration into smaller intervals that are easier to deal with. In this scenario, the duration (1 hour 32 minutes) can be broken down into 1 hour, 30 minutes and 2 minutes.

One at a time, add these to the start time, until you reach the end time.

1 hour 32 minutes

+ 1 hour   + 30 mins   + 2 mins

6:45   7:45   8:15   8:17

Ethan arrived in work at 8:17 a.m.

Robyn is going to a conference in Edinburgh, Scotland. Her train leaves London at 11:35 a.m. and arrives in Edinburgh at 3:53 p.m. How long is Robyn's train ride?

1 Identify what information is required to answer the question.

You are given the start time and the end time, so you need to find the duration.

2 Count up in minutes from the start time until you reach the nearest hour. Then count in hours until you reach 3:00 p.m. Finally, count on in minutes until you reach the end time, 3:53 p.m.

+ 25 mins   + 3 hours   + 53 mins

11:35   12:00   3:00   3:53

3 Add together the minutes and the hours to calculate the duration of the train ride.

25 mins + 53 mins = 78 mins = 1 hour, 18 mins
1 hour, 18 mins + 3 hours = 4 hours, 18 mins

Robyn's train ride was 4 hours, 18 minutes long.

Lucie ran a 10 km charity race in 52 minutes. She finished at 11:06, what time did she start?

1 Identify what information is required to answer the question.

You are given the end time and the duration, so you need to find the start time.

2 Count back 2 minutes from the end time. Then count back 50 minutes.
If 50-minute intervals are too difficult, count back in 10-minute intervals.

– 50 mins   – 2 mins

10:14   11:04   11:06

Lucie started her charity race at 10:14.

---

daydream
EDUCATION

Ali needs to pick up his daughter from school at 3:35 p.m. He has a half-hour dentist appointment at 2:20 p.m., and he has estimated that it will take 40 minutes to drive from the dentist to his daughter's school. Will Ali get to school on time to pick up his daughter?

1	Identify what information is required to answer the question.	You are given the start time, a desired end time and the duration, so you need to work out the actual end time.

2	Add half an hour (the duration of the dentist appointment) to the start time (2:20). Then add 40 minutes (the duration of the journey).	

If Ali's estimates are correct, he will get to the school at 3:30 p.m.; five minutes before the pickup time.

Practice

1 Kim is tiling his bathroom. He finished tiling at 11:55 a.m. but needs to wait for the adhesive to set before he can start grouting. The quick-drying tile adhesive he used takes 3 hours and 15 minutes to set. At what time can he start grouting?

_____

_____

2 (a) Kate got on the train at London Paddington at 6:42 p.m. She arrived in Manchester at 9:11 p.m. How long was Kate on the train?

_____

_____

2 (b) Kate drove home from the train station. She arrived home at 10:07 p.m. How long did the drive home take?

_____

_____

3 Liam has an interview at 3:15 p.m. He is meeting his friend for lunch beforehand. He has estimated that it will take him 35 minutes to get to the interview and 45 minutes to have lunch. What is the latest time Liam should arrange to meet his friend?

_____

_____

_____

daydream
EDUCATION

Timetables

A timetable is a chart that shows the times of particular events, such as transport departure and arrival times, or a student's lessons.

Train Timetable Example

The first column lists the stations that the trains stop at and depart from.

Each column represents a different train.

Station	Train 1	Train 2	Train 3
Swansea	09:40	10:32	11:15
Bridgend	10:10		11:35
Cardiff	10:40	11:25	11:56
Newport	11:15	11:57	12:27

If a train does not stop at a station, the cell is left empty.

Each row contains the times at which different trains depart from each station.

If Ed catches the 10:32 train from Swansea, what time will he arrive in Cardiff?

1 Look along the Swansea row until you reach the cell that contains 10:32.

2 Move down this column until you reach the Cardiff row. The time in this cell is 11:25, so Ed will arrive in Cardiff at 11:25.

Station	Train 1	Train 2	Train 3
Swansea	09:40	10:32	11:15
Bridgend	10:10		11:35
Cardiff	10:40	11:25	11:56
Newport	11:15	11:57	12:27

Eli wants to arrive in Newport before 12:00. What is the latest train he can catch from Swansea?

1 Look along the Newport row until you reach the last time before 12:00.

2 Move up this column until you reach the Swansea row. The time in this cell is 10:32, so the last train Eli can catch from Swansea is the 10:32 train.

Station	Train 1	Train 2	Train 3
Swansea	09:40	10:32	11:15
Bridgend	10:10		11:35
Cardiff	10:40	11:25	11:56
Newport	11:15	11:57	12:27

Austin is catching the 10:10 train from Bridgend. How long will it take him to get to Newport?

1 Look along the Bridgend row until you reach the cell that contains 10:10.

2 Move down this column until you reach the Newport row. The time in this cell is 11:15, so the train arrives in Newport at 11:15.

3 Calculate the difference in time to identify how long it will take Austin to get to Newport.

Station	Train 1	Train 2	Train 3
Swansea	09:40	10:32	11:15
Bridgend	10:10		11:35
Cardiff	10:40	11:25	11:56
Newport	11:15	11:57	12:27

1 hour → 5 mins →

10:10   11:10   11:15

daydream
EDUCATION

Creating Timetables

Timetables can be organised in different ways. If you're creating a timetable, ensure that you follow the instructions carefully and cover all eventualities.

Alisha is organising a football tournament for 5 football teams. She has two pitches that are available from 10:00 to 11:15. Each game will be 10 minutes long with a 5-minute break between each game. Create a timetable for the tournament below.

	10:00	10:15	10:30	10:45	11:00
Pitch 1	1 v 4	1 v 3	1 v 2	1 v 5	2 v 4
Pitch 2	2 v 3	2 v 5	4 v 5	3 v 4	3 v 5

Alisha could create a timetable like this for the tournament.

Practice

Station	Train 1	Train 2	Train 3	Train 4
Bath	03:13	03:43	04:13	04:43
Chippenham	03:24	03:54	04:24	04:54
Swindon	-	04:10	-	05:10
Reading	04:12	04:43	05:11	05:43

1 If Scarlett catches the 04:24 train from Chippenham, what time will she arrive in Reading?

2 Marcel got on the train at Bath. He arrived in Chippenham at 04:54. What time train did he catch?

3 Elliot's nearest train station is Chippenham. He wants to get to Swindon before 05:00. What is the last train he can catch from Chippenham that will get him to Swindon before 05:00?

4 Gabriela works at her local cinema. The cinema has three screens but one has broken. Help Gabriela create a film timetable below. All films need to be played twice. There must be a 15 minute break between each film and the same films cannot run at the same time.

The Wedding (105 mins)   Creepy Creatures (120 mins)

Frosty Fred (90 mins)   Crazed (120 mins)

	5.00	6.00	7.00	8.00	9.00	10.00	11.00	12.00
Screen 1								
Screen 2								
Screen 3	x x x x	x x x x	x x x x	x x x x	x x x x	x x x x	x x x x	x x x x

Tables

Tables organise and present data so that it is easy to interpret and make comparisons. Data is organised in columns and rows.

Tables can be used to display a wide range of data. They can help with budgeting, time-management and general organisation.

The table below shows the specifications of 3 different laptops.

Laptop	OS	Processor	Memory	Storage	Screen	Price
A	Windows 10	i5	8 GB	1 TB	15.6"	£599
B	OS X	i5	16 GB	500 GB	13.3"	£949
C	Windows 10	i5	32 GB	1 TB	15.6"	£799

Based on the information displayed in the table, which laptop would you choose?

Frequency Tables

Day	Visitors
Mon	94
Tue	106
Wed	182
Thu	143
Fri	203
Sat	221
Sun	194

A frequency table is used to record how often a value (or set of values) occurs. Frequency tables can be arranged in rows or columns.

These frequency tables show the number of visitors to a climbing centre during a week in February.

Day	Mon	Tue	Wed	Thu	Fri	Sat	Sun
Visitors	94	106	182	143	203	221	194

Collating and presenting this information will help the owners identify patterns and enable them to plan staff, to budget and to create forecasts for their business.

Mileage Charts

A mileage chart is a type of table that displays the distances between places.

To work out how far it is from Bristol to Oxford:

1. Move down the Bristol column until you reach the Oxford row.

2. The cell where the Bristol column and the Oxford row meet contains the distance.

Cardiff						
46	Bristol					
57	14	Bath				
73	40	37	Swindon			
106	72	70	30	Oxford		
67	39	52	35	48	Gloucester	
83	60	75	57	83	29	Worcester

It is 72 miles from Bristol to Oxford.

daydream
EDUCATION

1 Isaac is looking to book a holiday for 2 adults and 2 children. The table below shows the different packages available.

Resort Name: Tropical Palms			Board:	Self Catering	
	Adult Prices		**Child Prices**		
Nights	7	14	7	14	
Low season	£395	£695	£195	£395	
High season*	£545	£895	£395	£695	
*High season: 12ᵗʰ July – 31ˢᵗ August.					

1 (a) Isaac is considering going for 7 days in August. Calculate the total cost of the holiday.

_____

1 (b) Isaac is also considering going for 14 days in May. How much more would this cost than if he were going for 7 days in August?

_____

_____

2 Estelle runs a stall at her local football club. The table displays her sales for the last game.

2 (a) Estelle buys scarfs for £5 and sells them for £8. How much money did Estelle make on scarves?

_____

2 (b) Estelle makes £15 on a shirt and £21 on a jacket. Which item did Estelle make the most money from?

_____

Item	Quantity Sold
Scarf	120
Flag	16
Face paint	86
Pins	18
Shirt	49
Jacket	36

3 The mileage chart below shows the distances between various places in England.

3 (a) Barsha lives in Leeds. She has a college open day in Durham. How far does she have to travel?

_____

Hull

47	York			
61	25	Leeds		
66	61	37	Sheffield	
129	71	84	117	Durham

3 (b) Nina lives in York and Richard lives in Hull. They are both going to a football game in Sheffield. Who has to travel the farthest?

_____

_____

_____

Bar Charts & Pictograms

Bar Charts

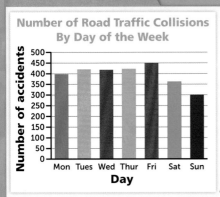

Number of Road Traffic Collisions By Day of the Week

A **bar chart** uses different-sized bars to represent data. When drawing bar charts:

- Give the graph a title.
- Always label both axes.
- Use equal intervals on the axes.
- Leave a gap between each bar.

Bar charts can be used to display qualitative and categorical numerical data.

Bar-line graphs use lines instead of bars.

1 According to the chart, on which day of the week are you most likely to have a road traffic collision? _____

Composite Bar Charts

A **composite bar chart** displays proportions, with each bar split into categories.

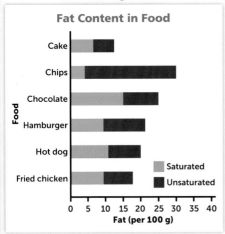

Fat Content in Food

Saturated
Unsaturated

2 Which food contains the most saturated fat?
_____

Dual Bar Charts

A **dual bar chart** displays two sets of data so it is easy to make comparisons.

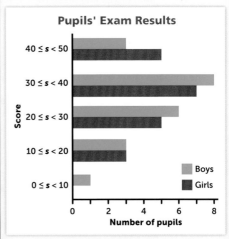

Pupils' Exam Results

Boys
Girls

3 How many boys scored more than 30 in their exam?
_____

daydream EDUCATION

Ice Cream Sales   = 40

Flavour		Frequency
Chocolate	🍦🍦🍦🍦	160
Vanilla	🍦🍦🍦	100
Strawberry	🍦🍦🍦	120
Mint	🍦🍦	60
Raspberry	🍦	20
Bubble gum	🍦🍦	80

A **pictogram** uses pictures to represent data.

All pictures must be the same.

4 If an ice cream costs £2.80, what was the total revenue from chocolate ice creams?

_____

_____

Practice

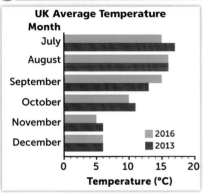

UK Average Temperature

The chart opposite shows average temperatures in the UK between July and December in 2013 and 2016.

1 (a) Which was the coldest month in 2016?

_____

1 (b) What was the monthly average temperature in September 2013?

_____

1 (c) What was the difference in average temperature between October and September in 2016?

_____

1 (d) In which year was the average temperature highest between July and December?

_____

2 Seren is a marketing executive for a clothing company. Her company's clothes are sold on two websites. Sales from each website are shown below. Create a composite bar chart to help Seren present this information.

Month	Website A	Website B
Quarter 1	£15,000	£20,000
Quarter 2	£15,000	£15,000
Quarter 3	£13,000	£17,000
Quarter 4	£25,000	£35,000

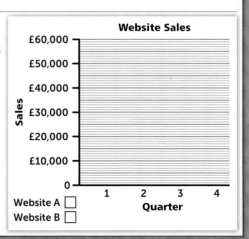

Website A ☐
Website B ☐

Line Graphs

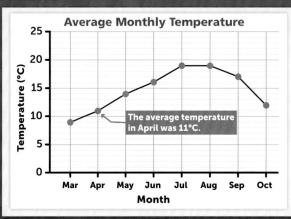

Average Monthly Temperature

The average temperature in April was 11°C.

In a **line graph**, data is plotted as a series of points that are joined with straight lines.

Line graphs are used to display continuous data and help show trends or change over time.

Always ensure your line graph has a title and that the axes are labelled and at equal intervals.

What was the average monthly temperature in June?

Real-Life Example

Line graphs can display multiple sets of data for comparison. In such instances, a key is needed to show what each line represents.

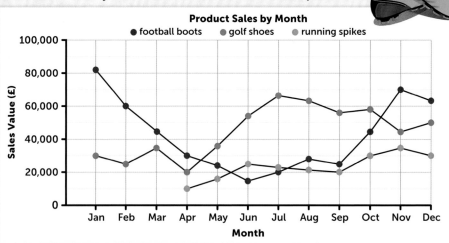

Product Sales by Month

● football boots   ● golf shoes   ● running spikes

Fin owns an online shoe store that specialises in sports footwear. The graph above shows the sales of his bestselling products. From the graph, you can infer that:

| He launched his running spikes in April. | Sales of golf shoes are best during the summer months. | Sales of football boots are best during the winter months. |

daydream EDUCATION

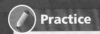
1 (a) The graph below shows how the value of a car reduced over time.
If Lilly bought the car when it was 3 years old, how much would she have paid?

_____

1 (b) Parker bought the car from Lilly for £5,000. How old was the car?

_____

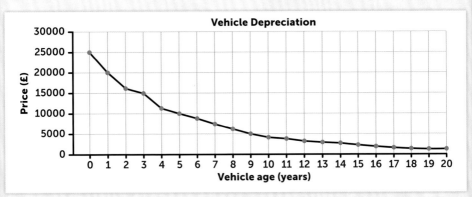

2 The table below shows the number of visitors to a soft-play centre over a 2-year period. Plot the figures on the graph paper below.

Year	Jan	Feb	Mar	Apr	May	Jun	Jul	Aug	Sept	Oct	Nov	Dec
1	762	842	1020	863	924	622	770	850	795	921	965	1011
2	1182	1056	1132	1094	978	724	789	945	856	1221	1306	1450

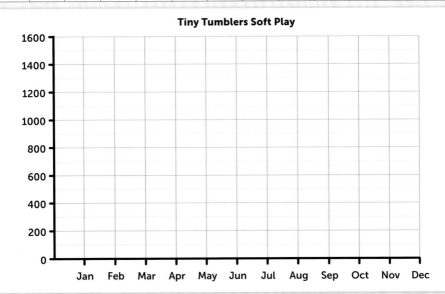

Pie Charts

A pie chart is a circular chart that is split into sections to show proportion. It is used to display categorical data.

Look at how the data from this frequency table has been displayed in a pie chart. The pie chart makes it easy to identify relative proportions of multiple classes of data.

Pupils' Summer Holiday Destination	Frequency
UK	21
Europe	34
America	5
Australia	1
Asia	3
Africa	6
Other	12
No holiday	14

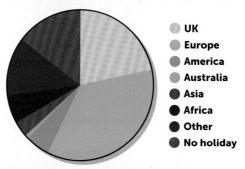

- UK
- Europe
- America
- Australia
- Asia
- Africa
- Other
- No holiday

The pie chart clearly illustrates that Europe was the most popular holiday destination.

Creating Pie Charts

The table below shows a group of 30 students' favourite sport.
Follow the steps below to create a pie chart for this data.

Step 1: In a pie chart, data is represented as a proportion of 360, as there are 360° in a circle. Therefore, to calculate the proportion for each person surveyed, divide 360 by the total number of people surveyed: 360 ÷ 30 = 12.

Sport	Frequency	Frequency × 12	Proportion of 360
Rugby	4	4 × 12 = 48	48
Football	8	8 × 12 = 96	96
Cricket	4	4 × 12 = 48	48
Netball	6	6 × 12 = 72	72
Swimming	3	3 × 12 = 36	36
Tennis	2	2 × 12 = 24	24
Hockey	3	3 × 12 = 36	36
Total	30	30 × 12 = 360	360

Step 2: To calculate the proportions for each sport, multiply their frequencies by 12.
4 × 12 = 48

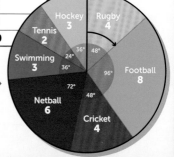

Step 3: Now that the sports have been converted to proportions of 360, the pie chart can be drawn.

Start by drawing a straight line from the centre of the circle to the edge.

Use a protractor to measure and mark the angles for each sport, and label them accordingly.

daydream
EDUCATION

Hannah works for her local water company. The average household in her area uses 96 gallons of water per day. The pie chart below shows how this water is used. Help Hannah calculate how much water is used for each activity.

To calculate the percentage value of an amount, convert the percentage to a decimal and then multiply it by the total amount.

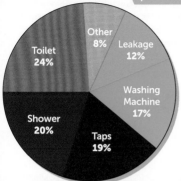

Types	Convert percentage to decimal	Multiply the total amount by the decimal
Toilet	24 ÷ 100 = 0.24	0.24 × 96 = 23.04
Shower	20 ÷ 100 = 0.20	0.2 × 96 = 19.2
Taps	19 ÷ 100 = 0.19	0.19 × 96 = 18.24
Washing Machine	17 ÷ 100 = 0.17	0.17 × 96 = 16.32
Leakage	12 ÷ 100 = 0.12	0.12 × 96 = 11.52
Other	8 ÷ 100 = 0.08	0.08 × 96 = 7.68

The totals for each activity should add up to 96 gallons.

Practice

1 Andi is compiling a report on energy production and usage. The pie charts below show the energy sources for this year and the year previous.

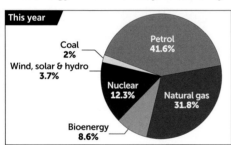

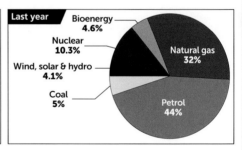

1 (a) The total energy produced this year was 125 million tonnes oil equivalent. How much of this was from petrol?

1 (b) The total energy produced last year was 120 million tonnes oil equivalent. How much of this was from natural gas?

1 (c) In which year was more energy produced from petrol?

Scatter Graphs

Scatter graphs are used to show how closely two sets of data are related. Correlation describes how the two sets of data are related.

Positive Correlation

When the **plotted points** go upward from left to right, there is **positive correlation**.

As one quantity increases, the other increases. As one quantity decreases, the other decreases.

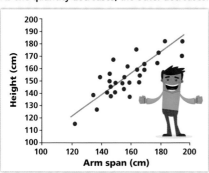

This graph shows that there is **positive correlation** between height and arm span. As height increases, so does arm span.

Negative Correlation

When the **plotted points** go downward from left to right, there is negative correlation.

As one quantity increases, the other decreases.

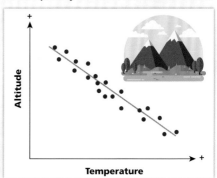

This graph shows that there is negative correlation between altitude and temperature. As altitude increases, temperature decreases.

No Correlation

When there is no linear relationship between two data sets, there is no correlation.

This graph shows that intelligence is not related to shoe size.

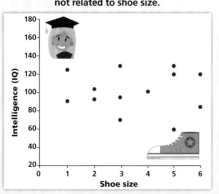

Line of Best Fit

A line of best fit is a line that is drawn through the centre of a group of data points.

When the plotted points are close to the line of best fit, there is **strong correlation**. When they are spread out on either side of the line of best fit, there is **moderate correlation**.

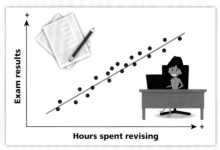

This graph shows a **strong positive correlation**.

Correlation and Causation

A correlation between two variables does not necessarily mean there is a direct cause-and-effect relationship between them.

Example >>> There is a strong positive correlation between number of cars owned and life expectancy. However, these variables are not directly related. Buying more than one car does not increase life expectancy. What other variable could be involved?

daydream EDUCATION

1 Jen works in a car garage. She is testing the stopping distances of various cars. The results are shown in the graph below.

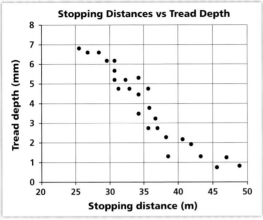

Stopping Distances vs Tread Depth

(graph: Tread depth (mm) on y-axis from 0 to 8, Stopping distance (m) on x-axis from 20 to 50)

GARAGE SERVICE

1 (a) Is there a positive or negative correlation between tread depth and stopping distance?

1 (b) The minimum tread depth for MOTs is 1.6 mm. How many cars were below this threshold?

2 The table below shows the exam scores for a group of students, along with the amount of time they spent revising in the two weeks prior to the exam. Plot the points on the graph below and determine whether there is a positive, a negative or no correlation.

Name	Revision Hours	Exam score
Kris	10	48%
Abbie	24	70%
Arjun	23	72%
Jakub	8	42%
Emily	32	90%
James	38	86%
Ayesha	30	74%
Jackson	35	84%
George	14	54%
Ellis	19	51%

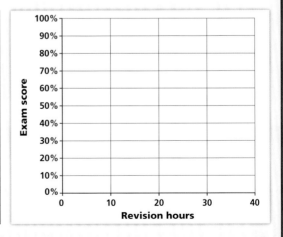

(graph: Exam score on y-axis from 0% to 100%, Revision hours on x-axis from 0 to 40)

Averages

An average is a measure of the middle value of a dataset. There are three main types of averages: mean, median and mode.

Mean

The mean is the sum of values divided by the number of values.

$$\text{Mean} = \frac{\text{Sum of values}}{\text{Number of values}}$$

Jessica is a self-employed interior designer. Her income over six months is shown below.

Month	January	February	March	April	May	June
Income	£1,979	£1,782	£2,109	£2,005	£2,274	£1,669

Jessica's mean monthly income over six months can be calculated as follows:

$$\text{Mean income} = \frac{1979 + 1782 + 2109 + 2005 + 2274 + 1669}{6} = \frac{11818}{6} = \begin{matrix}£1,969.67 \\ \text{(2 d.p.)}\end{matrix}$$

Mode

The mode is the value that occurs most often.

The average spend of customers in a bakery over one week is shown in the table opposite.

The modal spend in the shop is £0 – £5.00, as this is the amount that occurs most often.

Spend	Frequency
£0 - £5.00	137
£5.01 - £10.00	65
£10.01 - £15.00	104
£15.01 - £20.00	72
£20.01 - £25.00	14

Median

The median is the middle value when the data is arranged in order of size. If there is an even number of values, then the median is the mean of the middle two values.

The results of eight athletes in a 100 m track race are shown below.

Position	1st	2nd	3rd	4th	5th	6th	7th	8th
Time (seconds)	10.97	11.04	11.63	11.94	12.12	12.47	13.53	15.08

As there are eight values (an even number), calculate the median of the middle two values.

11.94 + 12.12 = 24.06 seconds
24.06 ÷ 2 = 12.03 seconds

The median time for the 100 m race is 12.03 seconds.

Range

The range is the difference between the lowest value and the highest value in a dataset. The monthly mean temperatures in Hull between July and December 2017 are shown below.

Month	July	August	September	October	November	December
Temperature (°C)	15.2	15.6	14.6	10.1	5.5	6.3

To find the range, subtract the lowest value from the highest value. 15.6 − 5.5 = 10.1°C
The range of mean temperatures in Hull between July and December 2017 is 10.1°C.

1 The table below shows the number of visitors to a cinema in a week.

	Mon	Tue	Wed	Thur	Fri	Sat	Sun
The Dark House	72	68	50	72	92	94	87
Explorer Emma	89	82	75	66	90	76	79
Flight 202	75	78	84	87	85	88	72

1 (a) What is the modal attendance for The Dark House for the week?

1 (b) What is the mean attendance for Flight 202 for the week?

1 (c) What is the median attendance for Explorer Emma for the week?

1 (d) What is the range of total visitors to the cinema each day?

2 Mallie is buying a new laptop. She is considering the online reviews for 2 different models. The reviews are scored out of 10 (with 1 being the worst and 10 the best).

Laptop 1	Review 1	Review 2	Review 3	Review 4	Review 5	Review 6
Performance	8	9	7	10	7	8
Ease of use	7	7	6	10	8	6
Value	6	7	6	10	7	9

Laptop 2	Review 1	Review 2	Review 3	Review 4	Review 5	Review 6
Performance	10	9	7	8	7	8
Ease of use	9	8	9	10	6	5
Value	10	7	7	9	6	7

2 (a) What is the median review for Laptop 1's ease of use?

2 (b) What is the mode review for Laptop 2's value?

2 (c) Overall, which laptop has better reviews?

Probability

Probability is used in everyday life to predict the chances of things happening.

Probability Is Measured on a Scale of 0–1

The probabilities of all outcomes add up to 1.

Unlikely
No rain for one week in the UK

Likely
Picking a heart, club or spade from a deck of cards

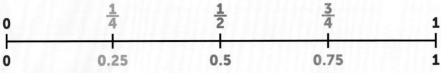

0	$\frac{1}{4}$	$\frac{1}{2}$	$\frac{3}{4}$	1
0	0.25	0.5	0.75	1

Impossible
Rolling a 7 on a dice

Even Chance
Tossing a head

Certain
Picking a red ball from a bag of only red balls

Estimated Probability = $\dfrac{\text{Number of Successful Events}}{\text{Total Number of Events}}$

The probability of scoring a 4 when rolling a dice is $\frac{1}{6}$.

$$P(4) = \frac{1}{6}$$

The probability of picking a club from a deck of cards is $\frac{1}{4}$.

$$P(\text{club}) = \frac{13}{52} \text{ or } \frac{1}{4}$$

Real-Life Example

Lisa is organising a raffle for a charity event. She has 80 raffle tickets, labelled 1 – 80. If a person picks a raffle ticket with a zero at the end, they win a prize. What is the probability that a person will choose a winning ticket?

1	Work out how many tickets will have a zero at the end:	10, 20, 30, 40, 50, 60, 70 and 80. There will be eight winning tickets.
2	Estimate the probability of choosing a winning ticket.	$\dfrac{\text{Number of successful events}}{\text{Total number of events}} = \frac{8}{80} \text{ or } \frac{1}{10}$

This can also be written as a decimal, 0.1, or as a percentage, 10%.

daydream
EDUCATION

Listing All Outcomes

Listing all possible outcomes of an event can help when calculating probabilities, making it less likely that outcomes are missed.

The table below lists all 20 possible outcomes of the two spinners.

	Red (R)	Green (G)	Orange (O)	Green (G)
1	1R	1G	1O	1G
2	2R	2G	2O	2G
3	3R	3G	3O	3G
5	5R	5G	5O	5G
1	1R	1G	1O	1G

The probability of spinning a 2 and a red (2R) is: $\dfrac{1}{20}$

The probability of spinning a 1 and a green (1G) is: $\dfrac{4}{20}$ or $\dfrac{1}{5}$

Practice

1 Jade has baked 120 pasties for a networking event. 50 of the pasties are corned beef, 40 are cheese and onion and the remainder are vegetable. What is the probability that a person choosing a pasty will pick a vegetable one?

2 (a) Mick is a quality-control assessor at a factory that manufactures mobile phones. The amount and colours of phones produced per day are shown below.

Mick picks a phone at random to test. What is the probability that the phone will be either gold or rose-gold?

Colour	Quantity
Black	40,000
Silver	30,000
Gold	10,000
Rose-Gold	5,000

2 (b) Altogether, Mick tests 300 phones and finds that 4 of them have faults. What is the probability that one mobile phone has a fault?

3 The probability of a bus arriving to its depot on time is 0.884. The probability of a bus arriving early is 0.05. What is the probabilty, as a percentage, of a bus arriving late?

Column Addition

It is not always possible to perform addition in your head. In such instances, column addition should be used.

Jasmine is planning a weekend break to Madrid. Everything she needs to pay for is shown below. How much will the weekend break cost Jasmine?

$$162 + 275 + 350$$

Flights - £162　　　Accommodation - £275　　　Spending money - £350

To solve this addition problem, follow the steps outlined below.

1 List all prices underneath one another, so that digits with the same place value (hundreds, tens, ones) are aligned vertically.

```
  h  t  o
  1  6  2
  2  7  5
+ 3  5  0
_____
```

2 When performing column addition, always work from **right to left**.

Add the numbers in the ones column first.

$2 + 5 + 0 = 7$

Write the answer underneath the numbers that are being added together.

```
  h  t  o
  1  6  2
  2  7  5
+ 3  5  0
_____
        7
```

3 Add the numbers in the tens column.

$6 + 7 + 5 = 18$

If the answer has two digits, the second digit, 8, is written underneath the numbers added in the tens column, and the first digit, 1, which represents 100, is carried over to the hundreds column.

Write the carried number here.

```
  h  t  o
  1  6  2
  2  7  5
+ 3  5  0
_____
     8  7
  1
```

4 Add the numbers in the hundreds column, and remember to include any carried numbers.

$1 + 2 + 3 + 1$ (the carried number) $= 7$

Write the answer underneath the numbers that are being added together.

$162 + 275 + 350 = 787$

So, Jasmine's weekend break will cost £787.

Remember to add me!

Remember to include the correct units in your answer.

```
  h  t  o
  1  6  2
  2  7  5
+ 3  5  0
_____
  7  8  7
  1
```

 daydream EDUCATION

Column Subtraction

A vehicle manufacturer has 468 employees. The company offers full-time and part-time positions. If 272 employees are full-time, how many are part-time?

468 – 272

To solve this subtraction problem, follow the steps outlined below.

1 List the number being subtracted, 272, **under** the other number, 468, so that digits with the same place value (hundreds, tens, ones) are aligned vertically.

$$\begin{array}{r} h \quad t \quad o \\ 4 \quad 6 \quad 8 \\ - \ 2 \quad 7 \quad 2 \\ \hline \end{array}$$

2 When performing column subtraction, always work from **right to left**.

Subtract the numbers in the ones column first.

$8 - 2 = \mathbf{6}$

Write the answer underneath the ones column.

$$\begin{array}{r} h \quad t \quad o \\ 4 \quad 6 \quad 8 \\ - \ 2 \quad 7 \quad 2 \\ \hline 6 \end{array}$$

3 Subtract the numbers in the tens column. If the top number is smaller than the bottom number, take 1 from the column to the left (hundreds).

Because 6 is smaller than 7, take 1 from the hundreds column. The 4 in the hundreds column becomes 3, and the 6 in the tens column becomes 16.

$16 - 7 = \mathbf{9}$

More on the floor? Go next door and get 10 more!

$$\begin{array}{r} h \quad t \quad o \\ {}^3\!4 \ {}^1 6 \quad 8 \\ - \ 2 \quad 7 \quad 2 \\ \hline 9 \quad 6 \end{array}$$

4 Subtract the numbers in the hundreds column, and write the answer underneath.

$3 - 2 = \mathbf{1}$

$468 - 272 = \mathbf{196}$

So, there are 196 part-time employees working for the vehicle manufacturer.

$$\begin{array}{r} h \quad t \quad o \\ {}^3\!4 \ {}^1 6 \quad 8 \\ - \ 2 \quad 7 \quad 2 \\ \hline 1 \quad 9 \quad 6 \end{array}$$

Addition and subtraction are opposite operations, so you can use addition to check your answers to subtraction problems. Add the answer (196) to the number that was subtracted (272) to see if it matches the original number: 196 + 272 = 468. ✓

Long Multiplication

It is not always possible to perform multiplication in your head.
In such instances, long multiplication should be used.

**An aeroplane can carry 232 passengers.
How many passengers can 6 aeroplanes carry?**

232×6

To solve this multiplication problem, follow the steps outlined below.

1 Write the smaller number underneath the larger number, so that digits with the same place value (hundreds, tens, ones) are aligned vertically.

$$
\begin{array}{ccc}
h & t & o \\
2 & 3 & 2 \\
\times & & 6 \\
\hline
\end{array}
$$

2 Multiply each digit in the top number by the bottom number. Always work from **right to left**.

$2 \times 6 = 12$

Write the 2 underneath the ones column and carry the 1 over to the tens column.

Write the carried number here.

$$
\begin{array}{ccc}
h & t & o \\
2 & 3 & 2 \\
\times & & 6 \\
\hline
 & & 2 \\
 & & 1
\end{array}
$$

3 Multiply the next digit, 3, in the top number by the bottom number, 6, and add any carried numbers.

$3 \times 6 = 18; 18 + 1$ (the carried number) $= 19$

Write the 9 underneath the tens column and carry the 1 over to the hundreds column.

Remember to add me!

$$
\begin{array}{ccc}
h & t & o \\
2 & 3 & 2 \\
\times & & 6 \\
\hline
 & 9 & 2 \\
1 & 1
\end{array}
$$

4 Multiply the next digit, 2, in the top number by the bottom number, 6, and add any carried numbers.

$2 \times 6 = 12; 12 + 1$ (the carried number) $= 13$

As there are no more numbers to multiply, the whole number can be written underneath.

$232 \times 6 = 1392$

So, 6 aeroplanes can carry 1,392 passengers.

$$
\begin{array}{cccc}
 & h & t & o \\
 & 2 & 3 & 2 \\
\times & & & 6 \\
\hline
1 & 3 & 9 & 2 \\
 & 1 & 1
\end{array}
$$

daydream EDUCATION

Gareth is a plumber. He purchases a van through a no-deposit finance agreement and pays monthly instalments of £430 over two years (24 months). How much will Gareth pay for the van in total?

Real Life Example 2

430 × 24

To solve this multiplication problem, follow the steps outlined below.

1

Rewrite the multiplication problem, so that the smaller number (24 months) is written under the larger number.

Multiply each digit in the top number by the bottom number. Always work from **right to left**.

$0 × 4 = 0$

Write the 0 underneath the ones column.

```
    h  t  o
    4  3  0
×      2  4
          0
```

2

Working from **right to left**, multiply the next digits in the top number by the bottom number, 4. Remember to add any carried numbers.

$3 × 4 = 12$
$4 × 4 = 16; 16 + 1$ (the carried number) $= 17$
Therefore, $4 × 430 = 1,720$

```
    h  t  o
    4  3  0
×      2  4
    1  7  2  0
       1
```

3

Before the top number can be multiplied by the next digit in the bottom number, 2, a zero needs to be added in the ones column. This is because the 2 in the bottom number actually represents 20.

It is **vital** that this step is performed or the answer will be incorrect.

```
    h  t  o
    4  3  0
×      2  4
    1  7  2  0
       1
          0
```

4

Now multiply each digit in the top number by 2. Remember to work **from right to left**.

$0 × 2 = 0$
$3 × 2 = 6$
$4 × 2 = 8$
Therefore, $20 × 430 = 8,600$

```
    h  t  o
    4  3  0
×      2  4
    1  7  2  0
       1
    8  6  0  0
```

5

Finally, use column addition to add the two products together.

$0 + 0 = 0$
$2 + 0 = 2$
$7 + 6 = 13$
$1 + 8 + 1$ (the carried number) $= 10$
$430 × 24 = 10,320$

Remember to include the correct units in your answer, e.g. £.

So, Gareth will pay a total of £10,320 for the van.

```
      h  t  o
      4  3  0
×        2  4
      1  7  2  0
         1
+     8  6  0  0
    1  0  3  2  0
    1
```

Short Division

It is not always possible to solve division problems in your head. In such instances, short division can be used.

Four friends are going travelling together. The total cost of the trip is **£8,192**. How much does each person have to pay if the costs are being split equally?

The number being divided is called the **dividend**. → $8192 \div 4$ ← The number by which the dividend is divided is called the **divisor**.

The answer to a division problem is called the **quotient**.

To solve this division problem, follow the steps outlined below.

1 Rewrite the division problem so that the **dividend** (8192) is written in a division bracket and the **divisor** (4) is written to the left of the bracket.

$$4 \overline{)8\ 1\ 9\ 2}$$

2 Short division is performed from left to right, so divide the first digit in the **dividend** (8) by the **divisor** (4).

4 goes into 8 twice: $8 \div 4 = 2$

Write 2 directly above the first digit in the dividend.

$$4 \overline{)\overset{2}{8}\ 1\ 9\ 2}$$

3 Divide the next digit in the **dividend** by the **divisor**. In this instance, 4 does not go into 1. Therefore, 0 is written above the division bracket, and the 1 is carried over to the next digit (9) to create 19.

$$4 \overline{)\overset{2\ 0}{8\ 1\ {}^{1}9\ 2}}$$

4 Divide 19 by the **divisor** (4).

4 goes into 19 four times (4 x 4 = 16) with 3 left over so:

$19 \div 4 = 4$ remainder 3

Write 4 above the 9 in the division bracket, and carry the remainder (3) over to the next digit (2) to create 32.

$$4 \overline{)\overset{2\ 0\ 4}{8\ 1\ {}^{1}9\ {}^{3}2}}$$

5 Divide 32 by the **divisor** (4).

4 goes into 32 eight times so: $32 \div 4 = 8$

Write 8 above the 2 in the dividend.

$$4 \overline{)\overset{2\ 0\ 4\ 8}{8\ 1\ {}^{1}9\ {}^{3}2}}$$

$8192 \div 4 = \textbf{2048}$

So, each friend has to pay **£2,048**.

Remember to include the correct units in your answer.

Multiplication and division are opposite operations, so you can use multiplication to check your answers to division problems. Multiply your answer (2048) by the divisor (4) to see if it matches the dividend: 2048 x 4 = 8192. ✓

daydream EDUCATION

Answers

Maths Skills

Estimating (Page 9)
1 (a) 24,000 – 13,000 = 11,000

OR 24,500 – 12,500 = 12,000

It can be estimated that there were 11,000 or 12,000 empty seats at Greenwood Town's last game.

1 (b) 15,000 + 3,000 = 18,000

24,000 – 18,000 = 6,000

OR 15,500 + 3,500 = 19,000

24,500 – 19,000 = 5,500

It can be estimated that there will be 6,000 or 5,500 empty seats at the next game.

Number

Addition & Subtraction (Page 11)
1 18,464 – 2,243 – 6,492 – 5,430 = 4299

There are 4,299 people in the remaining stand.

2 32 + 48 + 35 + 43 + 24 = 182

The school does not have enough places.

Multiplication (Page 13)
1 15 × 42 = £630

2 Apples: 104 × 5 = 520

Oranges: 64 × 4 = 256

Pears: 80 × 3 = 240

Lemons: 48 × 2 = 96

3 12 ÷ 3 = 4

4 × 40 = £160

Division (Page 15)
1 White rose: 92 ÷ 23 = 4

Purple freesia: 115 ÷ 23 = 5

Green pistache: 276 ÷ 23 = 12

Lilies: 138 ÷ 23 = 6

2 75 ÷ 24 = 3.125 (round down to 3)

30 ÷ 5 = 6

52 ÷ 16 = 3.25 (round down to 3)

3 × 6 × 3 = 54

Leo can pack 54 books in each box.

Negative Numbers (Page 17)
1 4 – 12 = –8°C

2 September: –2,310 + 1,300 = –£1,010

December: –810 + 1,090 = £280

Number Lines & Scales (Page 19)
1 320 ml **2** –6°C **3** 550 g

Fractions, Decimals & Percentages

Fractions (Page 20)
1 $\frac{3}{10}$ **2 (a)** $\frac{1}{5}$ **2 (b)** $\frac{2}{5}$

Fractions (Page 21)
1 (a)

Product	Total	Discount	Price
Radiator	3 × 79 = £237	237 ÷ 4 × 1 = £59.25	237 – 59.25 = £177.75
Pipes	1 × 26 = £26	26 ÷ 10 × 3 = £7.80	26 – 7.80 = £18.20
Pipe fittings	1 × 48 = £48	48 ÷ 10 × 3 = £14.40	48 – 14.40 = £33.60
		Total	£229.55

1 (b) 54 ÷ 6 = 9

9 × 5 = 45

45 customers rated Aston as excellent.

Fractions (Page 23)
1 (a) $\frac{12}{72} \overset{\div 12}{=} \frac{1}{6}$

1 (b) $\frac{28}{72} \overset{\div 4}{=} \frac{7}{18}$

1 (c) $\frac{18}{18} - \frac{7}{18} = \frac{11}{18}$

Adding & Subtracting Fractions (Page 25)
1 $\frac{1}{4} = \frac{5}{20}$

$\frac{3}{5} = \frac{12}{20}$

$\frac{5}{20} + \frac{12}{20} = \frac{17}{20}$

OR

$\frac{1}{4} = 0.25$

$\frac{3}{5} = 0.6$

0.25 + 0.6 = 0.85

0.85 = $\frac{85}{100}$ which simplifies to $\frac{17}{20}$.

2 1 ÷ 10 = 0.1, 1 ÷ 8 = 0.125, 1 ÷ 5 = 0.2

2 ÷ 5 = 0.40, 1 ÷ 8 = 0.125

0.1 + 0.125 + 0.2 + 0.4 + 0.125 = 0.95

Isla has used 0.95, $\frac{95}{100}$ or 95% of the container of car shampoo. $\frac{95}{100}$ simplifies to $\frac{19}{20}$.

Mixed Numbers and Improper Fractions (Page 27)
1 1 ÷ 2 + 8 = 8.5

8.5 ÷ 5 = 1.7

Isabelle needs to put 1.7 tonnes of top soil in each bag.

2 3 ÷ 4 = 0.75, 1 ÷ 4 + 2 = 2.25

1 ÷ 2 + 1 = 1.5

0.75 + 2.25 + 1.5 = 4.5

The journey took 4.5 hours, $4\frac{1}{2}$ hours, or 4 hours and 30 minutes.

Decimal Calculations (Page 29)
1 (a) 229.79 × 20 = £4,595.80

1 (b) 272.80 ÷ 20 = £13.64

1 (c) 4595.80 + 272.80 = £4,868.60

1 (d) 81.8 + 91.4 + 219.4 + 32.7 + 102.3 = 527.60

Nikita drove a total of 527.6 miles last week.

1 (e) 527.6 – 61.4 = 466.2

Nikita will be claiming for 466.2 miles.

Comparing & Ordering Decimals (Page 31)
1 The order of 100 m times from fastest to slowest is: 10.807, 11.024, 11.26, 11.49, 11.9

Rounding Numbers (Page 33)
1 Norway: 5,000,000

Iceland: 332,500

Denmark: 5,712,000

Sweden: 10,000,000

Finland: 5,503,100

Answers (continued)

2 Hairspray: £19
Shampoo & conditioner: £56
Hair dye: £150
Foil and meche: £35
Fuel: £200
Mia's approximate total costs: 19 + 56 + 150 + 35 + 200 = £460.

Percentages (Page 34)
1 (a) $220 \times 50 = 11,000$
$12\% = 0.12$
$11,000 \times 0.12 = £1,320$
1 (b) $72\% = 0.72$
$8,550 \times 0.72 = 6,156$
$6,156 \times 50 = £307,800$

Percentages (Page 35)
1 $24 \div 30 = 0.8$
$0.8 \times 100 = 80\%$
2 $23 \div 28 = 0.82$
$0.82 \times 100 = 82\%$
Roger has achieved his target.
3 5 stars: $280 \div 560 = 0.5$, $0.5 \times 100 = 50\%$
4 stars: $140 \div 560 = 0.25$, $0.25 \times 100 = 25\%$
3 stars: $84 \div 560 = 0.15$, $0.15 \times 100 = 15\%$
2 stars: $42 \div 560 = 0.075$, $0.075 \times 100 = 7.5\%$
1 star: $14 \div 560 = 0.025$, $0.025 \times 100 = 2.5\%$

Percentage Change (Page 36)
1 $184,000 \times 0.15 = 27,600$
$184,000 + 27,600 = 211,600$ Woodland's Water Park are expecting 211,600 visitors this year.
2 $9495 \times 0.22 = 2088.90$
$9495 - 2088.9 = 7406.1$
Li Na's car is now worth £7,406.10.
3 $\frac{23,400-18,000}{18,000} = \frac{5,400}{18,000} = 0.30 = 30\%$

Fractions, Decimals, Percentages (Page 38)
1 $1 \div 4 = 0.25$
2 $0.78 \times 100 = 78\%$
3 $2 \div 5 = 0.4$
$0.4 \times 100 = 40\%$
4 $0.52 \times 100 = 52$
$\frac{52}{100} = \frac{13}{25}$
5 $63 \div 100 = 0.63$
6 $\frac{80}{100} = \frac{8}{10} = \frac{4}{5}$
7 $\frac{9864}{15000} = 0.6576$
$0.6576 \times 100 = 65.76\%$

Fractions, Decimals, Percentages (Page 39)
1 $46 \div 100 = 0.46$
$2 \div 3 = 0.6\dot{6}$
$8 \div 10 = 0.8$
$86 \div 100 = 0.86$
So, the correct order is:
0.04, 0.46, 0.5, 0.6̇6, 0.8, 0.86 OR
0.04, 46%, 0.5, $\frac{2}{3}$, $\frac{8}{10}$, 86%

2 Shop A: $60 \times 0.3 = 18$
$60 - 18 = £42$
Shop B: $1 \div 4 \times 50 = 12.50$
$50 - 12.50 = £37.50$
Shop C: $1 \div 2 \times 80 = 40$
$80 - 40 = £40$
The dress is cheapest in shop B.

Ratio and Proportion
Ratios (Page 42)
1 (a) $3 + 2 + 1 = 6$
$2748 \div 6 = 458$
Bella: $3 \times 458 = £1,374$
Harry: $2 \times 458 = £916$
Rosie: $1 \times 458 = £458$
1 (b) $2 + 3 = 5$
$1388 \div 5 = 277.60$
Live sound technicians: $2 \times 277.60 = £555.20$
Lighting technicians: $3 \times 277.60 = £832.80$
1 (c) $8 + 8 + 12 + 20 = 48$
$864 \div 48 = 18$
Dave: $8 \times 18 = £144$
Ellie: $8 \times 18 = £144$
Dan: $12 \times 18 = £216$
Jade: $20 \times 18 = £360$
2 $15 \div 2 = 7.5$
$7.5 \times 5 = 37.5$
Katie needs 37.5 kg of sand.
3 $2 \div 5 = 0.4$
$0.4 \times 6 = 2.4$
Eliot can make 2.4 litres of squash.

Proportion (Page 44)
1 $\frac{14.85}{3} = 4.95$

$4.95 \times 10 = 49.50$
10 packs of acrylic nails would cost £49.50.
2 Spaghetti: $350 \div 4 = 87.5$, $87.5 \times 3 = 262.5$ g
Chopped tomatoes: $400 \div 4 = 100$, $100 \times 3 = 300$ g
Mushrooms: $90 \div 4 = 22.5$, $22.5 \times 3 = 67.5$ g
Minced beef: $500 \div 4 = 125$, $125 \times 3 = 375$ g
3 $26.85 \div 3 = 8.95$
$8.95 \times 2 = £17.90$

Equations and Formulae
Solving Equations (Page 47)

1 (a) $x + 11 = 21$	**1 (b)** $3y - 5 = 16$
$\quad -11 \quad -11$	$\qquad +5 \quad +5$
$\quad x = 10$	$\quad 3y = 21$
	$\qquad \div 3 \quad \div 3$
	$\quad y = 7$
1 (c) $\frac{m}{5} + 4 = 9$	**1 (d)** $\frac{24}{w} = 4$
$\qquad -4 \quad -4$	$\qquad \times w \quad \times w$
$\quad \frac{m}{5} = 5$	$\quad 24 = 4w$
$\qquad \times 5 \quad \times 5$	$\qquad \div 4 \quad \div 4$
$\quad m = 25$	$\quad 6 = w$

2 $3d + 25 = 403$
$\quad -25 \quad\quad -25$
$\quad\quad 3d = 378$
$\quad\quad \div 3 \quad\quad \div 3$
$\quad\quad\quad d = 126$
126 delegates are attending the conference.
3 $6p - 3 = 27$
$\quad +3 \quad +3$
$\quad 6p = 30$
$\quad \div 6 \quad \div 6$
$\quad\quad p = 5$
There were 5 plasterboards in a pack.
4 $(7 \times 12) - m = 79$
$\quad\quad 84 - m = 79$
$\quad\quad +m \quad\quad +m$
$\quad\quad\quad 84 = 79 + m$
$\quad\quad\quad -79 \quad -79$
$\quad\quad\quad\quad 5 = m$

5 stewards were missing.

Formulae (Page 49)
1 $320 \div 5 = 64$ km/h
2 Total cost = (monthly fee × no. of months) + setup fee
= $(14.99 \times 12) + 49$
= £228.88
3 Degrees Celsius × 9 = 5 (Fahrenheit – 32)
$\frac{\text{Degrees Celsius} \times 9}{5} = \text{Fahrenheit} - 32$
$(\frac{\text{Degrees Celsius} \times 9}{5}) + 32 = \text{Fahrenheit}$
$(\frac{32 \times 9}{5}) + 32 = \text{Fahrenheit}$
$(\frac{288}{5}) + 32 = \text{Fahrenheit}$
$57.6 + 32 = \text{Fahrenheit}$
$89.6 = \text{Fahrenheit}$

Shape and Space
Symmetry (Page 51)
1 **2**

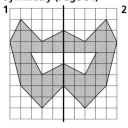
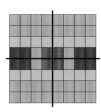

Solids and Their Nets (Page 53)
1

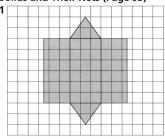

Elevations of 3D Shapes (Page 54)
1 Shape b is the correct side elevation.
2

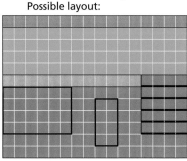

Plans (Page 56)
1 $10 \times 50 = 500$ cm
$20 \times 50 = 1000$ cm
Dimensions of the pool = 500 cm × 1,000 cm
or 5 m × 10 m
2 (a) $16 \times 0.5 = 8$
$4 \times 0.5 = 2$
$2 \times 8 = 16$ m²
2 (b) Table: $1 \div 0.5 = 2$ $\quad 2 \div 0.5 = 4$
Shed: $3 \div 0.5 = 6$ $\quad 2 \div 0.5 = 4$
Yes, Anna has enough room.
Possible layout:

Maps (Page 57)
1 Distance on map = 5.7 cm
Multiply by scale: $5.7 \times 1,000,000 = 5,700,000$
Convert to km: $5,700,000 \div 100,000 = 57$ km

Perimeter & Area (Page 59)
1 (a) $10 + 10 + 4 + 4 = 28$ m
1 (b) $10 \times 4 = 40$ m²
2 Circumference of circle = 2 × π × radius
$2 \times 3.14 \times 400 = 2512$
1 lap = 2512 m or 2.512 km
$10 \div 2.512 = 4$ (1 s.f.)
Saskia needs to run 4 laps of the park.
3 Area of circle = π × radius²
$3.14 \times (0.5 \times 0.5) = 0.79$ cm² (2 d.p.)
Katherine should tell the customer that the area of the pendant is smaller than 1 cm².

Area of Compound Shapes (Page 61)
1 Area of triangle = $\frac{1}{2} \times 14 \times (12 - 6.8) = 36.4$ m²
Area of rectangle = $14 \times 6.8 = 95.2$ cm²
Total area = $36.4 + 95.2 = 131.6$ m²
Paint coverage = $2 \times 10 \times 6 = 120$ m²
Shannon does not have enough paint.

2 (a) Area of room: $2 \times 12 = 24$ m²

$10 \times 5 = 50$ m²

$7 \times 8 = 56$ m²

$24 + 50 + 56 = 130$ m²

Cost of laminate wood flooring:

$15 \times 130 = £1,950$

2 (b) $12 + 8 + 7 + 2 + 7 + 2 + 12 + 12 = 62$ m

2400 mm = 2.4 m

$62 \div 2.4 = 26$ (2 s.f.)

Ryan will need 26 packs.

3 Area of rectangle: $15 \times 5.4 = 81$ m²

Area of semi-circle = $\pi \times (5.4 \div 2)^2 \div 2 = 11.45$ m²

Total area = $81 + 11.45 = 92.45$ m²

Cost of turf = 3×93 (rounded up) = £279

Kurt has enough money to buy the turf he wants.

Surface Area (Page 63)

1 (a) Existing packaging:

Area of rectangle: $2 \times 3.14 \times 2 \times 14 = 175.84$ cm²

Area of circles: $3.14 \times 2^2 = 12.56$ cm²

$12.56 \times 2 = 25.12$ cm²

Total area: $175.84 + 25.12 = 200.96$ cm²

New packaging:

Area of rectangle: $2 \times 3.14 \times 4 \times 6.5 = 163.28$ cm²

Area of circles: $3.14 \times 4^2 = 50.24$

$50.24 \times 2 = 100.48$ cm²

Total area: $163.28 + 100.48 = 263.76$ cm²

The new packaging requires more material as it has a larger surface area.

1 (b) Surface area of 1 face:

5 cm $\times 5$ cm $= 25$ cm²

Surface area of whole box:

25 cm² $\times 6 = 150$ cm² so, 150 cm² of cardboard would be needed.

Volume (Page 65)

1 Parcel A: $45 \times 38 \times 50 = 85,500$ cm³

Medium parcel label.

Parcel B: $\frac{1}{2} \times 16 \times 12 \times 28 = 2,688$ cm³

Small parcel label.

Parcel C: $\pi \times 11^2 \times 82 = 31,170.88$ cm³ (2 d.p.)

Medium parcel label.

2 Skip A: $\frac{1}{2} \times (0.91 + 1.82) \times 1.3 \times 2.6 = 4.6$ m³ (1 d.p.)

Skip B: $\frac{1}{2} \times (1 + 1.43) \times 1.76 \times 1.8 = 3.8$ m³ (1 d.p.)

Skip A will best meet Mark's requirements as skip B is too small.

Measurement

Measures (Page 67)

1 (a) $27,530 \div 1000 = 27.53$ km

$56.8 - 27.53 = 29.27$ km

Harry has 29.27 kilometres left to drive.

1 (b) $181,442 \div 1000 = 181.442$

$13,500 \div 181.442 = 74.4$

The lorry can carry a maximum of 74 pallets.

2 $640 \times 35 = 22,400$ ml

$22,400 \div 1000 = 22.4$ l

$22.4 \div 2.5 = 8.96$. Jenna's coffee shop has used 9 bottles of syrup in the past month.

Metric to Imperial Measurement Conversion (Page 69)

1 (a) Convert litres into gallons:

$55 \div 4.5 = 12.22$ (2 d.p.)

Multiply the cost per gallon by the number of gallons: $5.36 \times 12.22 = £65.50$ (2 d.p.)

1 (b) Convert miles to kilometres:

$65 \times 1.6 = 104$ km/h

2 Calculate the total number of pounds gained:

$0.75 \times 12 = 9$ lbs

Convert to kilograms: $9 \div 2.2 = 4.09$ kg

Add the weights: $4.09 + 93.44 = 97.53$ kg

3 Convert inches to cm: $205 \times 2.54 = 520.7$ cm

Ben should order 2×300 cm lengths of worktop at £150 each.

Time (Page 70)

1 (a) 4:05, or five minutes past four.

1 (b) 10:40, or twenty minutes to eleven.

1 (c) 10:55, or five minutes to eleven.

2 (a) **2 (b)** **2 (c)**

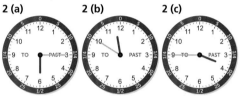

Time (Page 71)

1 (a) 3:20 a.m. = 03:20

1 (b) 12:05 a.m. = 00:05

1 (c) 7:38 p.m. = 19:38

2 $4:15 + 12:00 = 16:15$

$16:15 + 1$ hour $= 17:15$

Gabriela will not get to the cinema before the film starts. She will be 15 minutes late.

Time Intervals (Page 73)

+3 hours   +15 mins

1 11:55 ⌢ 14:55   14:55 ⌢ 15:10

Kim can start grouting at 15:10 or 3:10 p.m.

+18 mins   +2 hours   +11 mins

2 (a) 6:42 ⌢ 7:00 ⌢ 9:00 ⌢ 9:11

Kate was on the train for 2 hours 29 minutes.

−49 mins   −7 mins

2 (b) 9:11 ⌢ 10:00 ⌢ 10:07

Kate's drive home took 56 minutes.

−45 mins −35 mins

3 1:55 ⌢ 2:40 ⌢ 3:15

Liam should meet his friend at no later than 1:55 p.m.

Timetables (Page 75)

1 05:11   **2** 04:43   **3** 03:54

4 Possible layout of the film timetable:

	5.00	6.00	7.00	8.00	9.00	10.00	11.00	12.00
Screen 1								
Screen 2								
Screen 3	xxxx	xxxxx	xxxxx	xxxxx	xxxxx	xxxxx	xxxxx	xxxxx

Handling Data

Tables (Page 77)

1 (a) 2 × 545 = £1,090
2 × 395 = £790
Total cost: 1090 + 790 = £1,880

1 (b) 2 × 695 = £1,390
2 × 395 = £790
1390 + 790 = £2,180
2180 − 1880 = £300

2 (a) 8 − 5 = 3
3 × 120 = £360

2 (b) Profit from shirts: 15 × 49 = £735
Profit from jackets: 21 × 36 = £756
Estelle made the most money from jackets.

3 (a) 84 miles

3 (b) York to Sheffield: 61 miles
Hull to Sheffield: 66 miles
Richard has to travel the farthest.

Bar Charts and Pictograms (Page 78)

1 Friday   **2** Chocolate   **3** 8 + 3 = 11

Bar Charts and Pictograms (Page 79)

4 160 × 2.80 = £448

1 (a) November

1 (b) 13°C

1 (c) 15 − 10 = 5°C

1 (d) 2013: (6 + 6 + 11 + 13 + 16 + 17) ÷ 6 = 11.5°C
2016: (6 + 5 + 10 + 15 + 16 + 15) ÷ 6 = 11.2°C
The average temperature was highest
between July and December in 2013.

2

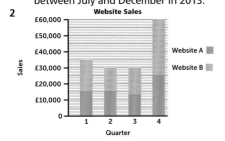

Line Graphs (Page 81)

1 (a) £15,000   **1 (b)** The car was 9 years old.

2

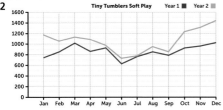

Pie Charts (Page 83)

1 (a) 125 × 0.416 = 52 million tonnes equivalent

1 (b) 120 × 0.32 = 38.4 million tonnes oil equivalent

1 (c) This year: 52 million tonnes oil equivalent
Last year: 120 × 0.44 = 52.8 million
tonnes oil equivalent. More energy was
produced from petrol last year.

Scatter Graphs (Page 85)

1 (a) Negative correlation. As tread depth decreases,
stopping distance increases.

1 (b) 5 cars

2

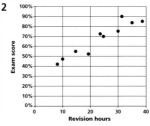

There is a positive correlation between exam results
and time spent revising.

Averages and Probability

Averages (Page 87)

1 (a) 72

1 (b) (75 + 78 + 84 + 87 + 85 + 88 + 72) ÷ 7 = 81

1 (c) 66   75   76   **79**   82   90   90
79 is the median attendance for Explorer Emma.

1 (d) Mon: 72 + 89 + 75 = 236, Tues: 68 + 82 + 78 = 228
Wed: 50 + 75 + 84 = 209 (low)
Thur: 72 + 66 + 87 = 225
Fri: 92 + 90 + 85 = 267 (high)
Sat: 94 + 76 + 88 = 258, Sun: 87 + 79 + 72 = 238
267 − 209 = 58
The range of total visitors to the cinema each
day was 58.

2 (a) 6, 6, **7, 7**, 8, 10   7 + 7 = 14   14 ÷ 2 = 7
The median for Laptop 1's ease of use is 7.

2 (b) 7

2 (c) Laptop 1:
Performance: 8 + 9 + 7 + 10 + 7 + 8 = 49
49 ÷ 6 = 8.2 (1 d.p.)
Ease of use: 7 + 7 + 6 + 10 + 8 + 6 = 44
44 ÷ 6 = 7.3 (1 d.p.)
Value = 6 + 7 + 6 + 10 + 7 + 9 = 45
45 ÷ 6 = 7.5
Laptop 2:
Performance = 10 + 9 + 7 + 8 + 7 + 8 = 49
49 ÷ 6 = 8.2 (1 d.p.)
Ease of use = 9 + 8 + 9 + 10 + 6 + 5 = 47
47 ÷ 6 = 7.8 (1 d.p.)
Value = 10 + 7 + 7 + 9 + 6 + 7 = 46
46 ÷ 6 = 7.7 (1 d.p.)
Laptop 2 has better mean reviews across all
review categories, except for performance
which is equal.

Probability (Page 89)

1 120 − 50 − 40 = 30 $\frac{30}{120}$ or $\frac{1}{4}$
The probability is $\frac{1}{4}$ or 0.25 or 25%.

2 (a) 10,000 + 5,000 = 15,000
40,000 + 30,000 + 10,000 + 5,000 = 85,000
$\frac{15,000}{85,000}$ or $\frac{3}{17}$ = 0.176 = 17.6%

2 (b) $\frac{4}{300}$ = 0.013 = 1.3%

3 1 − 0.884 − 0.05 = 0.066
0.066 × 100 = 6.6%

Index

Notes